Always Say Hello to Life

Also by James M. McMahon

The Price of Wisdom
Radical Self-Acceptance
In Praise of Psychotherapists

Always Say Hello to Life

How to let go of mother
and be your best self

James M. McMahon

Nepperhan Press, LLC
Yonkers, NY

Published by Nepperhan Press, LLC
P.O. Box 1448, Yonkers, NY 10702
nepperhan@optonline.net
nepperhan.com

PUBLISHER'S NOTE
The opinions expressed and the conclusions drawn
in this book are those of the author.

Printed in the United States of America

Library of Congress Control Number: 2009936426

ISBN 978-0-9794579-6-8

Cover art was licensed from Corbis.

For Lijuan

In every adult human there still lives a helpless child who is afraid of aloneness. When the conditions of social life are oppressive and antihuman, the adult is as alone in the world as a helpless child. This would be so even if there were a possibility for perfect babies and perfect mothers.

—Louise J. Kaplan, *Oneness and Separation: From Infant to Individual*

The scholar learns something every day, the man of tao unlearns something every day, until he gets back to non-doing.

—Lau-tzu (671 BC) quoted in Alan Watts, *Tao: The Watercourse Way*

Contents

Preface

THOSE WHO READ the first edition of this book, then titled "Letting Go of Mother," soon found out the book was not about abandonment, a fierce severing of lifetime ties. They found out it was about fine tuning the greatest of all loves, that between mother and child. It was about learning to live with all your emotions and learning to love yourself and to tolerate joy. It was in fact about creating a grown-up relationship with mom and becoming fully alive and awake. So I changed the title for this edition to be perfectly clear about this: "Always Say Hello to Life —how to let go of mother and be your best self." This little book is large with love: of mother, friends, lovers, self, and the entire universe.

Since its first publication in 1996 a lot has happened in the world. We have known two presidents and now a third. We have endured 9/11, the invasion of Iraq, Tsunamis, floods, earthquakes, and tornadoes of cosmic proportions. The world has gone into a prolonged financial recession. Yet as I studied what was in the first edition, I found its principles unchanged in their capacity to help free us to love better, to further our uniqueness, to more fully find joy and wonderful relationships. Others have told me this as well. There is much we can do to make the world better and to enjoy life more fully despite these tragedies over which we have little control. For whatever happens around us we must still negotiate our relationships with our mothers, a task all humans share and have always shared.

One Mother's Day (NY Times Op-Ed Page, 5/12/1996), August Wilson, author of the play, *Seven Guitars*, wrote:

1

Preface

Of all human relations, that of a mother and child is the most primary, the most fundamental. It is also sometimes the most complicated and is often, given the nature of human life, an embattled relationship.

Nevertheless, it is only when you encounter a world that does not contain your mother that you begin to fully comprehend the idea of loss and the huge and irrevocable absence that death occasions.

Like Red Carter (a character in *Seven Guitars* who is offered a choice of a red or white carnation on Mother's Day, and says: "I need me a red flower. My mother's still living. Even as I know it got to come to the day I wear a white flower, I hope it ain't no time soon."), I knew it would come to the day, Mother's Day 1983, when my brothers and sisters and I would wear a white flower for the first time. It is a rite of passage, daunting and profound, a moment of clarity in which the responsibility of your life is fully thrust into your hands. Up until that moment, whether you knew it or not, you had been as the gospel song puts it, "living on mother's prayer."

A world without the shelter and sustenance of mother's prayer is, when you first encounter it, an alien place. It is a world in which all the known references are dismantled and the cartographers labor day and night redrawing the maps. It is a world in which you are lost, like Hansel, in what D.H. Lawrence called the "dark forest of the soul," where you battle for light and clarity while looking for sharp and good directions.

If losing our mothers through the natural occasion of death is so devastating for most of us, how do we "let go" when she is still here? Actually, the kind of letting go I am speaking of has little to do with whether or not mother is still alive. The letting go I refer to has to do with the emotional attachment that we have to her, and this attachment transcends physical life.

My friend Jerry is eighty-five. His wife of many decades died last year. Recently, I asked him if he thinks of her each day. He pondered for a moment and then said, "No, but I think of my mother every day." When I ask people of all ages whether they think of their mothers, living or dead, all say yes. A large number think of her quite frequently; some, every day. So "Always Say Hello to Life—how to let go of mother and be your best self" is a study guide to becoming aware of your unending relationship with your mother whether you wear a red flower or white on Mother's Day. Our goal is to celebrate the thoughts and emotions and identifications with her which are loving and nurturing and at the same time to learn how to leave behind certain connections and fusions which keep us stuck and slow down our development into unique, free, and joyous selves.

1

Introduction

A BOOK ABOUT how to let go of mother is tough to write, mostly because I don't want to let go of my own mother. Nobody seems to.

When I would teach seminars on "psychological separation," it would take months for the participants, psychotherapists all, to relax this tension about their own mothers, to be open to understand what is in this little book. It is scary stuff. It is scary because as humans we have had a very long time in our relationship with mother to get convinced, at the deepest of levels, that we couldn't live without her. And as smart and sophisticated and accomplished as we may have become, this profound belief still lives in most of us, unhappily, to our detriment.

It is not because there is anything wrong with mothers. They run the full range from outstanding to terrible, as is true of any other human agency. Those of us who have more troubled persons as mothers perhaps have more trouble as a result. But even with the best there is trouble because it is the human condition. Our relationships with our mothers are the most beautiful and engaging of all human relationships; at the same time they are the most perilous to our spirit. They can be the greatest obstacle to our becoming the unique, once-in-all-creation persons that each of us is.

She is not to blame. Mother is just a fellow human being trying to extricate her spirit from her own mother. When we realize and accept that reality, we will be free.

I am going to try to accomplish much in a small space. I will try to persuade you that you are enmeshed in your mother to a much greater extent than perhaps you are aware. I will point out indications of this and suggest remedies. I will encourage you to be willing to experience all the emotions that will come up for you as you think about these things. I am going to emphasize self-centeredness, and shame, not in a blaming sense but to increase awareness. I am convinced that these inner emotional states are unavoidable; they are part of the human condition with all its limitations. You needn't blame yourself for any of these things. They are your lot in life. *Denying* their presence is the problem. I hope to help you be aware of them and to accept yourself as having them, as well as pointing out certain strategies for managing them.

I will speak of two major relationships that can help you grow out into the person you truly are. Notice I didn't say change. I don't think you need changing. None of us does. We need, rather, to jettison some ways we have learned to be, some attitudes and beliefs we thought to be essential to survival. When we do this we naturally return to our true selves, which are perfect. Committed long-term relationships as well as other friendships are major opportunities to do just this. We will look at intimacy and relatedness and see that they are not only fun and wonderful in themselves, but also marvelous chances to drop the baggage of the past and return to ourselves, to finish the unfinished aspects of our personalities.

I'm convinced that the only thing powerful enough to help us surrender the final self-destructive connections with our earliest caretakers is a relationship with a transcendent, a power greater than ourselves. Many people know this power as God, although that name carries such negative connotations for so many that I hesitate to use it. The crucial thing to realize is that *we* are not that transcendent, that there is a power in the universe beyond us. However you negotiate this issue is up to you. But don't dismiss it. Such a dismissal may be symptomatic of the very fusion with mother that this book is about.

5

I also want to say something about gender. Letting go of mother is a problem for all of us, females and males. Unfortunately our language doesn't permit me to employ both pronouns simultaneously. Sometimes I use the plural, but there are moments when the personal nature of what I have to say makes the singular more suitable. When I use the male pronoun, I am fully aware that what I speak of goes beyond gender. In fact, women have a particular struggle in becoming separate from mother because they have to become themselves at the same time as they must learn to be like their mothers in essential ways. The details of our separation unto ourselves differ somewhat because of our gender. But overall, the problems and challenges are more alike than different. We are all in this together. The same is true when I speak of the power greater than ourselves. The limitation of language forces me to assign a gender. The Spirit of which all of our spirits partake is, of course, beyond gender.

Letting go of mother may just be the next step in evolution. The psychological discoveries of the past century about separation and individuation may have been the preparation for this evolutionary phenomenon. But the evolution itself is a spiritual one. It is foreshadowed in scripture: "Whoever loves father or mother more than me is not worthy of me" (Mt 10:37). And substituting "letting go of" for "hating," "If anyone comes to me without hating his father and mother…he cannot be my disciple" (Lk 14:26).

For each of us to become who we truly are and co-create with the transcendent, we must let go of mother, at least the childish, dependent, all-encompassing involvement that most of us have with our mothers.

In the most primitive of times, in the most primitive of individuals, mother worship is pandemic. We are all called to move beyond this involvement and replace "oneness with mother" with radical self-acceptance and oneness with all.

2

Withdrawal Pains

THE BEST KEPT secret that I know of is the power of mother —not the power that mother has over her dependent children, but rather the power we invest in her as adults so that we do not have to live our lives. We joke about it, complain about it, sentimentalize it, but we all participate in a conspiratorial lie. It is not cute. The enmeshment most of us have in our mothers is malignant. It eats away at us. It limits what we are. It obviates joy.

The most intense, profound, humanly absorbing experience each of us has had and will ever have is with her. We all know this, but few acknowledge consciously the depth of feeling of this involvement or the pervasiveness of its influence in all aspects of our lives at all times and for always. No one is finished with mother. Your analyst, in his infinite wisdom, is not finished with mother. The priest in his pulpit, the guru in the lotus position before a thousand devotees, the supreme court justice writing a landmark decision, is not finished with his mother. No one is— ever.

The universal name for her is "mama," the first word spoken for most of us, the last for many. Those having experience with people of advanced age in institutions know the eerie sound of the call for mama in the darkness of the night. In a very real sense our entire life, the totality of our conscious existence, has reference to her.

The other day, sitting in the park, I noticed a young woman, not more than twenty or so, chewing gum and blowing bubbles.

In her care was a little boy of two or three, calling her mama. She was attentive and warm, but as she blew another bubble, I realized how little she knew about life and even about what she meant to that little fellow. Later I noticed him gaze at her when she was occupied with something else. It was a look of devotion and worship that he will seldom if ever give to any other. This young boy was deeply, madly, inexorably, impossibly in love.

The reason we feel so strongly about mother is that we woke up to her, and believed from that moment, if not before, that she was *absolutely essential to our staying alive*. This was the deepest of beliefs. And we loved her for our lives. With her we first experienced terror and surcease from that terror. We have never forgotten.

We humans are the greatest of all living things. We are able to love, to create, to remember, to dream. But we must also grapple with difficult issues. We will die. Those we love will die. Where did the world and life as we know it come from? Is there a God? Is he like us? Do we have a responsibility toward him? Why do we so often hate each other and kill each other? Why, even, am I the way I am and why do I do the things I do? What is going to happen to me? We are born fearful.

It doesn't appear that any other living creatures besides us have to figure these things out. The result of this is that we are mixed bags. We have great strengths, yet we have great weaknesses, too. And our relationships with our mothers are instances of this complexity. But from the beginning we had deep need of her.

The reasons we are "mixed bags," capable of the most generous and also the most horrendous acts, geniuses and yet often lost, are three: (a) our extremely *long*, dependent *childhood*; (b) our *consciousness* of what is happening around us from our earliest moments, and our making conclusions and forming *deep beliefs* from the teeniest of perspectives; (c) the *frailty* of our *parents*, for they were limited, too, and often treated us inconsistently and sometimes hurtfully. And so we are blemished

—all of us. It is our nature. We must be patient with ourselves, must always have compassion for ourselves.

Time flies. The older you get, the faster it flies. The younger we were, the slower it passed. Childhood took a long time. The childhood of humans is long anyhow—eighteen years or so. But in *experienced* time it is much longer. I think of it as about one hundred years. And all that time we were dependent on the "grownups" for food, shelter, protection, education, guidance, love, affection, self-concept, and more. We depended on many adults: presidents, pastors, neighbors, school crossing guards, Mr. Rogers, baseball stars, movie stars, doctors, teachers, aunts, uncles, cousins, brothers and sisters, grandmother and grandfather, father and mother—whom have I left out?

And through it all, first and foremost, from the beginning of *our* time and even before, we depended on mother. We depended on her for so long and for so much. She was bound to us by the profoundest of human tendencies, the love of one's young. And we were bound to her by gratitude and utter dependence which blended into the deepest and richest love we humans know. Sometimes we wanted to get away. More often we lived in fear that we might—or someday might have to.

From the moment of birth and our terror-stricken attempts to catch our breath and suck onto her again, the part of us that was ordained to be our uniqueness has been fighting it out with the part of us that wants to stay "one with mommy."

And for so long. Sometimes we stayed with her; sometimes we rebelled. Sometimes we held her hand and explored the world, both of us happy. Other times we wanted nothing to do with her. More often we paid great attention to her because it became very important to please her; our lives, it seemed, depended upon her approval. But we also loved her dearly.

Our love and our need kept us watching her, listening to her, smelling her. Early on it was taste and smell and the texture of her skin. Then, as we could make her out and hear her voice, we watched and listened.

What good students we were! We fixated on her as if our lives depended on it, and we loved her madly—all this for years and years, as we grew and learned the world and our bodies, and mastered new skills. Through it all she was there, watching us too, as we watched her. Watching, watching, watching. Learning, learning, learning. All we learned, all those hundred years, we learned with her or deliberately away from her, but rarely unmindful of her, somewhere inside of us.

We did what we were told to do for the most part, and did not do what we were told not to do. We learned more in those years than since. Much of it is claptrap. And, most important, we learned what we could learn and what we couldn't; what we could think and what we couldn't; what we could do and what we couldn't. Finally, we learned what was permissible to feel emotionally and what was not, and even if it was permissible to feel at all!

What wasn't told us directly we sensed. And we imitated. Watch the play of small children and you see the extent of the beliefs, attitudes, emotions, and values that are handed down unquestioned from parent to child. As we became more and more ourselves, those selves were profoundly riddled with mother, in our psyche and spirit. Then who is our true self?

During the dependent, loving, passionate years that we were looking and learning, we were also making judgments about what was happening around us. We were little philosophers; quick takes were made, and the deepest of beliefs were formed, never to be questioned. Reality was to be understood forevermore in the context of these beliefs. The world was to be shaped and formed and understood in a way consistent with them. Anything that threatened these deep beliefs was terrifying. People even learn to kill to preserve them, and surely to hate and nourish prejudices.

This is an instance of our peculiar human dilemma. Each characteristic of ours which sets us apart and above other living things seems to have a downside. No other species has consciousness, at least to the extent that we do. Yet because of our long childhood, we become aware of so much that we can't understand, and we tend to conclude things that are often incorrect, or at odds with the way nature actually works. We often wind up with a strange take on reality.

And if this were not enough, those who raise us suffer from the same disadvantages. The best of parents also have had inordinately long psychological childhoods and have spent hundreds of psychological years making decisions, often with faulty judgment, about how the world works and about *their* parents who themselves have had to wrestle with the same set of circumstances. Most mammals have mothers who provide for them in an instinctual preordained way that meets their needs perfectly, and when it is time for the offspring to go out on their own the parents just leave! No going over to a grandmother's for Sunday dinner or pay the price of guilt. We humans spend the rest of our lives making sense of our childhoods.

Some of us have not had the best of mothers. Some have suffered great abuse by troubled persons who expressed their madness in brutality, both physical and emotional. The children of such mothers have special trials as they negotiate life with scars and unresolved emotional trauma in their bones. For them, becoming their true selves, separating from the hurtful parent, is especially hard because it is a maddening reality that those who hurt us most are often the most difficult to leave, though we may put miles and years and even death between them and ourselves.

A more subtle version of damaging mothering is when the child is not truly "seen" by the mother. On the surface everything may seem all right, but within the psyche of the child is a profound insecurity which shows itself in excessive self-preoccupation. This narcissism covertly but deftly keeps children wed to their mothers by the creation of a web of emotional blindness which closes them off from real healing and loving relatedness.

Some of us, on the other hand, have had wonderful mothering. Someone once said that what children need most is someone to be crazy about them. Some mothers are crazy about their children and because of good fortune in their own lives are able to communicate this clearly to them. These offspring have an easier time in letting go of mother and becoming clearly themselves. They have a wonderful peer-like relationship with parents. These relationships are ones of love and respect and honor but not fusion. They seem rare but beautiful.

Still others are somewhere in between. The child gets a hefty amount of attention, for example, but mostly stemming from the mother's ambition or her own psychological needs. These children may grow up entitled, perhaps accomplish extraordinary things, but suffer the fallout of such maternal ambition, often having difficulty in personal and sexual relationships.

Most of us have had what the great English psychiatrist Winnicott calls "good enough" mothering. We have had mothers who have loved us and cared for us pretty much the best they knew how. Lord knows they had their foibles, and Lord knows we were affected by them, but they were not mean, and they meant well and they gave us a lot. All of us have been misunderstood and neglected, too. Despite the great range in this quality of care each of us has received, we all have the following in common:

1. We were dependent for what seemed an extremely long time.

2. We were aware of what went on, and we drew conclusions about what happened. Based on this we formulated "strategies," conscious and unconscious, about how to negotiate life, particularly our relationship with mother.

3. The best of mothers have had some disasters in their own upbringing which they brought to their mothering, and this impacted us.

(There are instances where the biological mother may not have done the mothering. Sometimes it was the father. In any

12

event father is the second crucial person for most of us and may even be felt as the most important influence. The relationship between mother and father and how it influences our fusion with each is also fascinating. Sometimes anger at mother covers surreptitious designs on father; sometimes anger at father obviates our studying the full implications of our relationship with mother. Other books will have to handle these matters. But if you are weighing these things in your head perhaps you are concerned with blame—who is really at fault—and this book is *not* concerned with blame. It is concerned with compassion. It is nobody's fault. It is the human condition. Know the truth, how your relationship with mother still affects you, and have mercy.)

In a sense these facts are no big deal. That's just the way it is for us humans. If anything, they should just encourage us to be compassionate. But fear makes us want to hold on, rather than be compassionate. The trouble really comes from our making a pact to stay enmeshed with mother, one way or another, to stem this fear. It is generally a secret pact, secret sometimes even to ourselves.

Regardless of the quality of the mothering we received we all must pass from "oneness with mother" to "oneness with ourselves." And each step forward, as we follow the imperatives of our spirit, is marked by ambivalence. We want to go, we need to go, we must go, but we want to hold on, too. The incarnation called childhood was about her, and we loved her wildly and gratefully, and now we must let her go to become fully ourselves. This is the central challenge of being a human being. But letting go of mother is truly hard for us, and these are the reasons:

1. We love her dearly, unlike any other love before or since. Who wants to leave such a love? How sad it feels. How sad it is.

2. Deep in our bones we have a belief that we can't survive without her, that she will protect us, even from death. Some of us believe that she knows more about what is good for us than even we do! We trust her more than we trust ourselves. How frightening it is to let go of her, the first Higher Power we know, and know so intimately.

3. Paradoxically, our earliest attempts to make sense of all this typically were marked by guilt and, even more powerful, by shame. These emotional states are hard to yield; they seem to exist in our cells, and in an odd way they keep us connected to their source. They won't go away simply because we tell them to. Much of the time we are not even aware of these feelings or we consider them to be our essential and inevitable lot. They become "chronic affects," a sort of familiar emotional state, an inner atmosphere that we grow accustomed to and eventually are reluctant to leave, much as a prisoner who becomes institutionalized and is terrified of returning to the outside world.

4. We feel responsible for *her*. Often the secret pact we had with her included a promise that we would take care of her and ensure her happiness forever. To do this it is essential that we be a certain way and never change. How can we betray her?

5. This witches' brew of sadness, fear, guilt, and shame leaves us with an anguish we are loath to feel. We may even have been ordered *not* to feel it. But if we don't feel it we can never fully move on. What a spot we are in!

Despite our best intentions we find ways of staying enmeshed. We may physically leave; we may even be aware of being angry at her. But only by going through the cauldron of all our feelings about her can we become free. And each of us resists this. When our spirits move us in the direction of psychologically separating, we begin to feel these emotions and we wonder why. The reason is that we are mourning. In fact, everyone in the whole world is mourning, and most are denying it.

Few will speak of this grief. It is considered immature. We live in a world where we are not permitted to speak of our sadness in growing up and moving on, abandoning our relationship with mother, at least as we knew it. Yet, signs of sadness and wanting to hold on are everywhere: the athlete greeting his mother on television; the vocalist who tells the world "I owe it all to Mom"; the terrified soldier crying for her in the foxhole during combat; the grieving aged woman calling out for mother in the silence of the night.

"Mommy and I are one." Does this desire ever leave us? How can it? Yet we are supposed to be the big boys and girls. The model presented to us was that of the brave little John-John as he saluted his president-father's bier. This we are told is the ideal. But we are all sad; we are all grieving. And models such as this prevent us from helping each other.

It is the human condition to be in conflict between that part of ourselves that deeply wants to grow into the unique, once-in-eternity-person each of us is, and that frightened little child in us that wants to stay attached to mommy. This fearful struggle is not shameful. It is the way it is for us. Be compassionate toward yourself. We have within us a strong, compelling psychological tendency to stay "fused" with mother, and if we are to be free, we must become more aware of what this means, and just how this tendency functions within us.

In the April 19, 1991 edition of the Berkshire, Massachusetts, *Eagle* was the following item:

DEAR ABBY: Please tell me if I am right or wrong. My daughter-in-law's brother, "Bob," was married last week, and I was invited to the wedding. It was a big social event, and one of the most beautiful weddings ever held in our cathedral.

My daughter, "Lisa," was not invited, and now she's mad at me because I went. She thinks I should not have gone because she wasn't invited. Abby, there is no reason why Lisa should have been invited—she's not related to Bob, and I am related only through marriage. Also she's never even met the bride. Do you think she's justified in being angry and insulted over this? Now she hates me because I attended the wedding.

Lisa is in her 50s and I am in my 80s.

HURT IN BROOKLYN

Lisa and her mother are somewhat "fused." Psychological fusion is a mechanism of the psyche that keeps certain persons "merged" with each other. Each is not fully a separate or independent person, even though that may not be apparent at first glance. It's vitally important that we get a precise understanding of what fusion "looks like" so we can recognize it in our own lives. Let me spell out precisely what I mean when I use the concept "fusion."

A person may be said to be "fused" when some aspect of his uniqueness, individuality, and independence is merged with another and thereby lessened. What are the dimensions of uniqueness, individuality, and independence that are compromised when a person "fuses"?

1. A person's freedom to *think*, and to think whatever he thinks without rules or restrictions or excessive or fearful mindfulness of another's attitudes toward his thinking or the content of his thinking.

2. A person's freedom to *feel all emotions*, and to feel whatever he feels without rules or restrictions or excessive or fearful mindfulness of another's attitudes toward the fact of his feeling emotion or the content of his emotion.

3. A person's freedom to *understand the world* through his own eyes and form opinions about the nature of reality and that which he values, and to do so without rules or restrictions or excessive or fearful mindfulness of another's attitudes toward his own perceptions and beliefs, or even the fact of his taking to himself the right to his own perceptions and beliefs.

4. A person's freedom to *act* in a way he needs to, or ought to, or wants to, without rules or restrictions or excessive or fearful mindfulness of another's attitudes toward his acting or the nature of his acts. It is up to him to decide in this matter. If his act is bad for him, reality will discipline him soon enough.

5. The realization that one's thinking, feeling, perceiving, valuing, and behaving are not the result of another, nor the cause of another's state of being or welfare. While one may be

conscious of the opinions, emotions, attitudes, values, behaviors, and welfare of another or others in making his decision, his behavior is not an automatic consequence of that understanding, conscious or unconscious, or of affects or emotions generated in response to this awareness, such as guilt and shame, but rather a free act, determined by himself.

Psychological fusion is a difficult concept to grasp. If my words sound a little like a legal brief here, please forgive me. It is because I want to be as clear as possible. Stay with me. Reread this section. It is very important. You can change your life if you deeply grasp what I am speaking about here. The key notion to grasp is that psychological fusion refers to the *deep belief that the thoughts, feelings, perceptions, values, or behavior of another are contingent on your own thoughts, feelings, perceptions, values, and behavior. Similarly, it is the tendency to regulate, consciously or unconsciously, your own thoughts, feelings, perceptions, values, and behavior with those of another.* There's a good chance that something like this notion explains why Lisa was threatened by her eighty-year-old mother's independent behavior. Today we might refer to her attitude as "codependent." Codependency refers to an internal psychic setup wherein one's self-esteem and sense of safety depend on pleasing or making happy another at the expense of one's own healthy needs. This is the tendency of many of us. And it is a very human tendency. It may be what we were taught that love is. On the wall in a room on Ellis Island is the 1985 memory of Felici Taldone, an Italian immigrant in 1924: "I left my mother (in Italy). You cry for your mother all the time, so I wrote a letter to my mother from Ellis Island. I told my mother I got off, I got a job…and it made my mother strong."

Being fused is such a familiar experience and even so comforting for many of us that the prospect of not being fused, of being psychologically separate, may be very frightening. We may think we will not be able to love anymore or be loved. Do not think for a moment that getting free of fusion and becoming more yourself will make you less loving! If there is one thing I

17

can guarantee you, it is this: The more you become YOU, the unique person you are, the more love you will have to give everyone, including mom.

I am inviting you in this reflection to consider your life: to think of your spirit, and evaluate how it moves and how free it is, and where you might be stuck. I am suggesting that you observe how you think and feel and behave, that you notice how your connection to mom may unwittingly be holding you back. This has to make you feel "crazy." Stop for a moment and notice how you are feeling. What emotions are you aware of this very moment? What thoughts are running through your mind? Do you feel any physical discomfort? Do you have an urge to do something? Notice your breathing. Is it rapid? Are you experiencing shortness of breath? Take a moment, be conscious of what you are feeling and take a few deep breaths. I feel this way a lot, and others who are reading this will feel the same way. It's OK. There's no danger. It's a little scary because it's unfamiliar. Most of us have been discouraged from knowing the great inner world of our emotions. Take a few minutes, close your eyes, and breathe.

A friend of mine who was dying from AIDS once said to me: "Relinquishing control is the task of the spiritual warrior." What a brave and powerful statement, I thought. If we intend to become aware of the ways our fusion with mother has strangled our impetus to growth, we will have to yield to our inner experience, and most of that will be the feelings, emotions, or affects that we have felt from birth but which may now be largely buried in our psyches or bodies or muted by all sorts of self-defeating behaviors and habits.

It's amazing to me how much confusion there is about emotions, even among professionals. Therefore I am going to present a list of emotions that a respected expert accepts as encompassing. The list is provided by Sylvan Tomkins and is reported in a wonderful and thorough book by Donald Nathanson.

With only a couple of exceptions, each innate affect is given a two-word group name, the first indicating the mildest form in which it may be seen, the second representing its most intense presentation. The positive affects are *interest-excitement* and *enjoyment-joy*; the neutral affect is called *surprise-startle*; and the negative affects are *fear-terror, distress-anguish, anger-rage, dismell, disgust,* and *shame-humiliation.* Each may be regarded as a pattern of expression, a specific package of information triggered in response to a particular type of stimulus. (D. Nathanson, *Shame and Pride: Affect, Sex, and the Birth of the Self.* New York: W.W. Norton, 1994, p. 59)

Even though our inner atmospheres may sometimes seem to be comprised only of vague apprehension or graying dullness, below that is some variation of these emotions. Many, perhaps most of us, have been strongly discouraged from feeling feelings, and so the prospect of it may be frightening. "Don't get emotional," we were admonished; we learned to apologize for "getting upset." But our emotions are absolutely crucial to our existence. We have them for very important reasons. They provide the color of life, but, even more important, they provide us with *vitally necessary information about reality.* If we are very angry about something, for example, we must understand the nature of the world that is eliciting this anger so we can come up with the best response. As we get to know our way around the secret world of our feelings, we may discover that there are different layers of feelings. Anger sometimes covers sadness. The pain we feel deep down at the suffering of another and our helplessness to do anything about it may lead to impatience or anger. We may also have several different feelings simultaneously. We could be angry at the refusal of a person to take care of himself, and at the same time feel some compassion for his inability to do so. Studying feelings is a great adventure.

"It's too confusing," we might say. But it's really not. Actually, it is fascinating, much more fascinating than a play or movie or TV drama. Sometimes I think our fascination with dramatic portrayals of life is a substitute for our observing and living in our own inner experience. Each of us has wonderful scenarios going on inside us, complete with all the staging and sets, representing our deep feelings. We need look no further for stimulation and excitement. Each of us is far more interesting than any canned stuff. But we have been scared off, told not to feel. As a result we waste a vast part of our life and experience.

It only seems confusing because to know what we truly feel means we will learn a lot about the truth of our worlds, like the necessity to let go of mother in order to become truly ourselves. Sometimes events are just so powerful that we yield to our grief and "break down." Even in the face of the most tragic of events, though, we often freeze and feel nothing. This does not mean we are not having a reaction. It means that we are managing to suppress it. Yet despite our best efforts to avoid it we often feel sadness. Much of the unaccounted-for sadness we know, even the mild depression, is the result of mourning for mother. This may be what happens to us when we meditate, when we feel lonely; the reason we tend to overeat, overdrink, oversex, over anything, is often our way to temper this sadness.

The whole world is grieving. You are not alone. So much of life is separation from mother. Withdrawal is always going on— physical, mental, emotional, even spiritual distress. It is inevitable. It is our nature, yet we generally come to the erroneous conclusion that there is something wrong with *us*. We feel shame because we are not happy. We punish ourselves because we are in pain. Much of our fear, sadness, shame, and guilt stems from our need to surrender to the reality of our hurt and loss, and from our knee-jerk attempts to not know this, not feel it, not realize that we are all, in some way, scarred. Just about all of our emotional problems as adults are the result of unresolved enmeshments with mother. It's all right. That's the way we are. Have compassion.

Tragically, we generally suffer in silence by ourselves, filled with shame that we are suffering, flailing about for someone or something outside ourselves to relieve us from this anguish. The Latin verb from which the word anxious comes is *angere*, to strangle. No matter how outgoing we may be, how involved in the world, there's a part of each of us that is strangling, gagging on suppressed feelings, and most of these have to do with leaving mother. The terror goes all the way back to the moment of birth when for a split second we thought we might indeed strangle, possibly die.

The technicians of our birth were absorbed in the mechanics of saving our life, not in our inner experience. Through much of our life we have never learned to let go of this tension, to express the bodily manifestations of feelings. Typically, those around us were also too frightened to be very receptive. Later we learn not to feel at all, and, if we do, to feel shame and to cover up the rainbow of our emotional landscape. We have had no chance to process the feelings of mourning at each stage of our early life. They were too scary—perhaps for mom as well. And so we learn well to hold tight, to reign ourselves in, and, most of all, to stay in control.

If you form the intention with me to observe your life, you will start feeling again, and there will be some mourning. The pain of mourning is like the ache of deeply massaged muscles that have been frozen in the stasis of fright. When those muscles become relaxed once again, the pain returns, to be felt and to dissipate as the deferred healing takes place.

So it is with our self. We bend ourselves out of shape to protect an archaic relationship with mother, one which no longer serves our spirits. And when we let loose of it our spirit aches— sometimes intensely. And we want to back off. But if we don't, we will pass through it—guaranteed—and the healed spirit will thrive. The reality is that as we become less stuck, the more of ourselves we become. We do not change so much as we *return*—return to our true spirit which we have abandoned over the years out of our fear of losing mother and fear of life itself.

Thinking about these things, or anything I say in this book, will not create any new bad feelings. Anything you may feel as a result of this reflection you have felt before. Only now we will reflect on these things lovingly, and together we may help you release them.

There are a few points it helps to keep in mind as you embark on this adventure.

1.   There is a difference between feelings, thoughts, and behaviors. They are distinct. They are not the same.

2.   It is extremely difficult to "change" feelings *directly*. Some things that we do, such as going to the beach, may ordinarily result in happy feelings. Other things, such as overtime at the office, may be counted upon to make us miserable. But, generally, feelings seem to have a life of their own, they seem to go and come with little conscious control. Sometimes we feel great although we are in terrible circumstances. More often we feel out of sorts in situations that "should" make us happy. Understand that there is little you can do to consciously control your emotions. Feelings come and go; they run through us, like a river flowing to its source. The good news is that they will change for the better *on their own* if we do not do something out of panic to perpetuate them. We needn't fear them.

3.   Feelings do not force us to *do* anything. There is no essential or inevitable behavior that accompanies a strong emotion. You can be enraged and not have to punch anyone. You can be wildly attracted to someone and not have to reach out and touch. You can do what needs to be done regardless of your feelings. Actually it is better *not* to act on them. The purpose of feelings is to provide us with information. It is our thought processes that help us to formulate "right acts." Feelings are our friends. They are gifts to us from God. Accept and enjoy them.

4. Part of the confusion about feelings is that there is more to us than meets the eye. Our psyches are like symphonies with many, many lines of music/feelings going on inside us at the same time, most of which we may be scarcely aware of (except in our dreams). But they are playing their music anyhow, and sometimes they provide little melodies that may seem mighty strange to us! Actually they are tunes that always move in the direction of our spirits, but since they are not under control of our conscious egos, we are wary of them. They can never do us harm. If left to their own devices, they move us on the road to health and joy despite our best efforts to the contrary.

And so I urge you to yield. There is nothing to fear. There is no danger in feeling. On the contrary, there can be great danger in not knowing your feelings, for they will come out in one way or another: in self-destructive behavior, in anxiety or depression, in addiction or illness.

Breathe deeply and step into your feelings. Experience them, work with them, surrender to them. Wrap yourself up in them. Don't try to figure them out. Immerse yourself in them. Discover that your feelings are friends. Trust your spirit.

As confusing and frightening as it may be initially, to step inside the world of your own emotional life is the beginning of freedom. For our feelings are who we truly are. They are the stuff of our response to life. They are much more important than thoughts. Thinking is very important, but thinking is just the means to an end. Feelings, having heart, is to be alive. And if you don't have that, what do you have?

Feelings are also the key to wresting back our self from the grip of our earliest caretakers. Sometimes there is sadness, but soon there is ever-growing joy.

3

Growing Out

ON THE SOUTHERN part of Long Island there are many miles of Atlantic Ocean beach. My surfer nephew tells me that this area comprises one of the most beautiful beaches in the world—no faint praise from someone who has settled in Hawaii. My family loves this place. We were lucky enough to spend a week or so there each summer for many years. They were spectacular times.

Each year a newspaper article would appear warning swimmers about riptides, sometimes called sea pusses. Occasionally, due to an irregular constellation of sand on the ocean bottom, there would be a short strip of shoreline which didn't follow the rules of the rest of the ocean. Step into the water at this point and you might be whisked away out into the ocean in a split second. Fighting it was useless. In fact, it was dangerous. The sea was not to be bested, and the swimmer who failed to acknowledge this quickly exhausted himself and was swallowed up. The newspapers warned us of this. They instructed us to look for the telltale signs of a rip, the discoloration and sandiness of the water, the small signs of turbulence. We were particularly wary of this because of our four small children. The water was always inspected before we set down our blankets and the digging with shovels and pails commenced in earnest.

The advisors of the signs and dangers of the sea puss always made the same suggestion, which was so hard to accept because it seemed to go against human instinct. They adamantly insisted that if you should get trapped in this bizarre undertow, it was essential to go with it, not fight it, and as soon as it had escorted you beyond the waves it would release you, guaranteed, and you could make your way back to the shore, or let the incoming tide do it for you. You would wind up on land unharmed, but perhaps some miles down the shore. To resist was certain death. And every year provided proof.

I learned a lot at the beach. I learned, for example, that when an enormous wave approached, it was best not to stand there and scream or even turn and attempt to drag my water-encased legs to the shore. Many scraped bellies taught me this completely. But to this day, at the moment of truth, I have an ever so slight resistance to putting my head down and diving into this gigantic wall of water. I do, and when I bob up on the other side, I am surprised that it truly worked. My survival by this means is a cause of wonder each time. Such is the power of human narcissism.

I want the world to work the way I want it to work, and when it doesn't I am miffed, and I try to force matters. I try to make it go the way I want it to go. The beach is such a wonderful teacher. I am convinced that anyone who spends a month on the beach with an open mind will be transformed. Far away from the man-made buildings and airplanes and self-made notions of how the world works, or how we make it work, you can just sit and watch. Every single day, day in and day out, the tide comes in and out, in and out. Each morning light sneaks up on you. All life on the beach rustles. On the beach you can see it, hear it, smell it. It gets inside you.

And at night, sitting with your arms around your knees, a sweater between you and the rising winds, you let yourself be aware of the coming to an end of this cycle, the dimming of the light. All living things respond. After a few days, your mind is emptying. The power of the regularity and the beauty kicks in. Your heart begins to beat in rhythm with the waves, just as women who live together tend to menstruate at the same time. You identify with the sandpipers scurrying along the shore, wishing for them to slow down and relax. It is hard to be an atheist on the beach as the sun goes down. When you are on the beach it gets harder each day.

Nature always wins, and the wisest among us know that, and find ways to cooperate. But we are easily seduced by the idea that we can *do*, that we can master. It has been our bête noire from all time. Genesis tells us that we can have it all if we acknowledge our limitedness and leave to the transcendent One what is his. To not eat of the tree of knowledge of good and evil; to live with mystery; to learn humility—it seems to be our fate to repeat our mistakes over and over again.

It is not our fate, but it is our nature because we are fused with mother, our first transcendent. This profound connection with her leads us to believe, in the deepest of places within us, that we can do anything. Regardless of the health or quality of our relationship with her, our early "oneness" with her has left us with this kind of self-centeredness. We have overcome our terror by maintaining our childlike notion of her unlimited power and protection through all sorts of psychological tricks and deals. The stronger our fusion with her, the more an underlying grandiosity lurks, even if we are manifestly self-deprecating. This is the "ego" that the ancients have been telling us about.

We may have fought this "oneness with mother" in our youth as our spirit struggled to express itself, but as we stepped out on our own as young adults, the fear of life soon conspires to incline us to the old ways. We have been in a struggle from the beginning between that part of ourselves, our spirits, which wants to express its unique destiny in the world, and that part of us that wants to stay fused with mother. We are all, each one of us, somewhere on that continuum from "oneness with mother" to "growing into ourselves."

How this world works is so wonderful. It never ceases to fascinate and overwhelm me with its beauty, its harmony, and its power. I'm especially interested in the beginning of life, so I'm captivated by how the newborn of any species negotiates its early days on earth, its relationship with mother, how it learns, literally, to stand on its own feet. The horse-like wildebeests of the African plains are an example. Hours after birth, while the herd is temporarily stopped for grazing and watering, a newborn calf staggers like a drunken sailor on wobbly feet, negotiating gravity and balance, to find nourishment, eliminate, and discover its political position in the herd. In the background, biding their time, are jackals, lingering. They surreptitiously wait for the herd to move on, hoping there will be some stragglers, some babies unfit to move with the pack. The newborn wildebeest has only a few hours to get its land legs, master all the skills necessary to keep up, and survive. Most do, though some do not, proving the wisdom of the jackals waiting.

The drama we humans are born into is psychological as well as physical and rests particularly on our capacities to communicate with each other. Because of the enormous size of our skulls, we are born with relatively immature development of our bodies and nervous systems. As a result, we are totally dependent for an extremely long period of time. It's another of those peculiar dilemmas we humans seem prone to. Our skull must be large enough to house the most complex computer in the universe. As a result, the physical mechanics of the birth process demand that we come out of the mother prematurely, with an extremely limited capacity to get along on our own. If the rest of our bodies had sufficient time to develop so that we could become more rapidly independent, the skull would be too large to pass through the vaginal canal.

To compensate somewhat for this dilemma, nature has provided us with a face comprised of an enormous amount of muscles, more than any other animal, so that we may communicate our needs and discomforts as quickly and powerfully as possible. Ensuing is a subtle dance between mother and child, the baby employing all aspects of its emerging

27

capabilities with each grimace and gurgle, and the mother receiving her offspring with every sense and sensitivity with which nature, life experience, and a good heart have equipped her. In the first hour after birth the newborn is alert and fixated on its mother, and the mother is mesmerized as well. They look at each other and form the most profound bond possible. From that moment the mother is taking her baby into a place not yet alive in her, and from that same moment the baby is watching with its entire being. The infant actually has the capacity from birth to imitate its mother's gestures and expressions, and it does. After an hour or so of this, they fall off into deep sleep, exhausted both from the trip and from the meeting. How shall their hearts ever be disentangled?

Who would want to leave such a connection? Unfortunately, the human condition does not always allow our bonding to be so positive. The possibilities for miscues and misfirings are enormous, and, sadly, inevitable. This complicated inter-dependency, while necessary for survival, will take a lifetime to work out. For as all the loving is going on, the brilliance of our potentialities for consciousness already has us starting to form opinions and philosophies about what is transpiring, and these "philosophies" are inevitably often incorrect and certainly always incomplete.

The spirit that leads the wildebeest to run fearfully and hesitatingly with the pack pushes for expression in us as well, but it has a formidable opponent, not merely in external danger, but in the fusions that we form from the beginning of our lives and continue to maintain, reinforce, and create in the new editions of our old enmeshments. For we determine from that first moment that we need them to survive.

This, then, becomes the task of life: to disentangle ourselves from the enmeshment with mother which has been our experience from the moment we first "woke up." For we woke up to her. That loving moment, so beautiful and so humanly moving, and so essential to our survival, contains within it not only the best about us and about

28

life but also the greatest challenge each of us will ever face. No other living thing has to deal with this. This is our destiny both as members of the human species and as the unique person that each of us is.

In a sense all adult life is recovering from childhood and all the moments, happy and not so happy, that bound us so deeply together with mother. Wherever we are *stuck* in our life is where we are fused with her. Our troubles are the result of erroneous ways we have developed to perpetuate this original fusion. It is not your fault that you got somewhat stuck. It is not mother's either. It is the human condition. It has most to do with the weird set of circumstances in which all humans find themselves. But you can be free. I urge you to consider this truth and to ponder committing yourself to return to the person you were before all the "deals" were made.

To the extent that we are enmeshed, we suffer. The suffering can take many forms. You can see them all around you, but you probably would not connect what you see with unresolved enmeshment with mother. I'll briefly describe some of these patterns of suffering. You will relate to some; others will seem foreign to you. They are the stuff of everyday living, ours and those around us. They all stem from unresolved fusion with mother.

Some of us learn to be as much like mother as possible. We mimic her behavior. We hold her opinions. We feel the way we believe she wants us to feel. We may even feel *what* we think *she* feels. We may be careful to do what she wants, to avoid doing what she would criticize. We defend her against anyone. In the extreme, some would even kill to protect her "honor." Anything or anyone outside the family may be deemed dangerous. We overvalue authority. We have childlike trust that if we are "good," someone will always take care of us.

But the ways we stay enmeshed are often much more subtle. Some of us develop obsessive thought patterns so as to not feel anything spontaneous or unpredictable. We might not think much at all. Or we might have deep beliefs about all aspects of life and love and never question them, even though they originated in early childhood. We often base our entire lives on these beliefs and will fight or avoid anyone who might challenge them.

Perhaps we carry around within us moods or feelings that are painful but carry the reassurance of the familiar—the chronic affects we spoke of above. We may worry, feel guilt and shame, be depressed or angry much of the time, or only feel what we were told was "appropriate" to feel. Some of us turn our suffering into physical pain; others have bodily preoccupations.

Some of us become perfectionists in the belief and vain hope that if we manage to do things perfectly, we will please our parents and ensure their love forever. Some of us develop what mental health practitioners call "symptoms": dysfunctional feelings or behaviors that disable us somewhat in coping with life. We may turn to addictions, ways of avoiding the experience of our anguished self—food, drugs, alcohol, sex, gambling, relationships, work. I personally don't consider to be a form of "sickness" the ways we learned in desperation to solve the conflict between the demonic tendency to stay merged with mother and the push of our spirits to grow out into our self. We are trying, screaming out in our suffering with the hope that perhaps someone will hear. But you are not "sick," no matter how troubled you feel. You are *stuck*, and you deserve to find less painful ways to solve this riddle of our humanness.

Others of us feel that the only way we can emotionally separate from our parents is to denigrate everything about them. We become absolute rebels, denying all appreciative and loving feelings. We live with chronic underlying rage. We may have little contact with them. But this attempt at solving the problem keeps us more enmeshed than ever. It is impossible to become emotionally free from someone you hate.

In general, remaining fused leaves one "hungry." Not being filled up and nourished as only a psychologically separating person can be, there is a constant yearning, a *chronic avariciousness* that cannot be satisfied. This shows itself in greediness, a sense of never having enough, and its consequences, a lack of gratitude and a lack of generosity. Such persons can never say "thank you" for fear of being further depleted or becoming "vulnerable" to the demands of others. To thank another would be, for these folks, to feel in their debt.

Envy is hell on earth. It poisons our very soul. We suffer when we observe the happiness of others and compulsively accumulate for ourselves alone, yet nothing works, nothing satisfies. It is as if we are wedded to a mother with empty breasts. And only in taking the chance of letting her go will we receive the nurturance that is in the universe.

Our relationships are frequently characterized by the blurring of the boundaries between partners. We may stay enmeshed with mother and isolate ourselves from all others and not have relationships. Or we may involve ourselves with others but re-create our earliest fusions with whoever stumbles into our life. We may go to any extreme to control our partners and those around us. We may perfect the victim role, or we may bully others either overtly, by yelling or menacing or threatening to leave, or more subtly by our very suffering and depression.

Some of us may be unable to confront or criticize mom or those who now play her role in our life. Even as adults we may be anxious lest she abandon us. It may be hard for us to have values and opinions different from hers. We may feel responsible for her thinking, her emotional state, even her bad behavior. ("I must have done something to make her behave so badly.") Even though you are helpless to do anything, you may anguish over her problems and suffer with her or for her. This is part of the secret pact. We stay connected by believing we are essential to mother's well-being. The safety we feel in such a psychological arrangement may seem to justify the deprivations and abandonment of our spirit.

Growing Out

There seems to be no end to the ways we humans have created to stay enmeshed in mother! Each of us has figured out so many ways. You have no more of them than I do or anyone else does. It is our nature. Develop compassion for yourself.

There is one more crucial thing we must keep in mind. Despite our suffering, the many problems we have, the difficulties we seem not to overcome, the bad self-concept— underneath it all pulses our *egos.* As we are enmeshed with mother, so we are self-centered, even though we may be beating ourselves up all over the place and it looks to all the world that we don't care for ourselves at all. This has been our problem from the beginning of time. Sages have been railing at us about our "egos," our self-centeredness, at every moment of history and in every culture. Each religious tradition speaks of it. "Help me, O Lord, to get rid of the 'I' that stands between you and me," prays the Muslim.

Some of us are *extremely* "I-centered." Doctors even consider the extremes of narcissism a mental disorder. But it is merely the apex of what we all suffer from. And suffer we do—in hurt feelings, in obsessive comparison with others, in lack of peace, in difficulty even in reaching out to the transcendent One. It is no fun being self-centered. And self-centeredness stems from fusion with mother. It is not our fault. Regardless of the quality of that relationship, it was special to us, and we have a strong tendency to hold onto the specialness even if we reject much of the rest of it. It is our nature.

In addition to the trouble which comes with just being alive, sickness, the death of loved ones, betrayal by others, and so much more, all of us seem destined to struggle with some variation of emotional baggage having at its root our difficulty in letting go of mother. But we can lighten our load. It is possible to suffer less and be less afraid. We can give our spirits room. For the rest of this chapter I am going to describe a simple (though not always easy) approach to becoming aware of and relinquishing the remnants of our no longer necessary fusions.

As is true for the person caught up in a sea puss, the first thing we need to do is: *absolutely nothing.* This notion is very hard for us humans to grasp. Our tendency is to *do.* But remember that we are not so much interested in changing as we are in *returning* to our essential self. Much of what we *have* been doing in our lives has been based on misperceptions of the nature of reality. In large measure, we have been living in a fusion-distorted reality. But reality is like life on the beach. It has clear rules; it is simple. It doesn't need our philosophies. It needs our clear vision. You needn't do anything. Breathe. Observe. Notice. You don't have to understand precisely the connection between your fusion with mother in a logical and linear way and the way you are suffering. You don't have to analyze anything. Intellectual knowledge may come later. It will be interesting, but it is not necessary for the healing and separation to occur.

All we need to do at this point is to *intend* to find a way back to the way things are, to release the ways we have been fused, and let ourselves grow naturally. It is not so much that we need to fix ourselves.

One of my coworkers told me recently that she was afraid of becoming unglued. We need to become a little unglued, I think. Most of us have been glued into an awkward emotional position. We need to let the glue melt a bit in order to return to a more natural shape. We won't fall apart. We have an emotional skin around us. We will just naturally rearrange.

I have found over the years that there are three central ingredients in this business of "growing out" or, more accurately, "returning" to our natural self. If you dig deep enough into any successful healing or therapeutic approach, you will find these three, though no one has identified them quite in this way. They are simply: *intention, observation,* and a self-acceptance so profound that I call it *radical self-acceptance* (RSA).

If you are willing to consider the possibility that you are more connected with mother than is good for you, or that you are suffering and don't quite know why, or that you are stuck in behaviors that fail to make you happy but you can't seem to move beyond them, then a reflection on these ingredients for growing out may be helpful to you. But remember: the important thing is not to *do* anything at this point but rather to "sit still" and be receptive to parts of you that have been sleeping.

This is not a matter of being active or passive. Rather, it has to do with which part of us will do the acting. Typically, it is our ego-motivated, "I can do it" part, the part of us that strives to be "in control," that prompts our actions. But here I am urging you to sit still and wait, *actively* wait, for the message from somewhere deep inside you, from the spirit. It will definitely come to you if you will be patient.

And while you wait you can reflect on what you want. How do you want to be? What are you unhappy about in yourself? What would you like changed? Don't think of changing others. That's a dead end and a terrible waste of your finite energy. Focus entirely on what you can do by yourself. Second, think long and hard and *tentatively* about what you want for yourself. As a psychotherapist I have noticed that what people want changes over time. Actually, it is more a matter of their discovering what they *truly* want rather than changing their minds. Much of the inability to effect change in ourselves has to do with our not being clear about just what it is that we want or want changed. Without clarity of *intention*, the whole process is doomed to failure.

But be tentative about your intentions. They might change. Expect that. It's no big deal. Be very patient with yourself. Gently release self-criticism. Then begin to do the second thing: *observe.* Become a "watchperson" of your life. Don't try to fix anything; don't try to change anything. Just observe. You will notice that you are frequently critical of yourself. Observe that, too. Be aware of it, and be aware of when you criticize yourself for criticizing yourself. Just notice. Most of all, try to have the courage to let yourself see all there is to see. There is nothing about you that would interfere with your becoming all that you are destined to be if you acknowledged and accepted it. I urge you to have faith in this right now.

Observation is a condition of gentle witness. It is no more than seeing what is—no more and, hopefully, no less. Try not to editorialize, to engage the voices that evaluate us as we watch. Actually, what is frightful or painful about what we discover are mostly the evaluations we make. "I would like to murder my boss," we discover. Fright and pain rush in. We deny the thought. We rationalize it. We shame ourselves. Or, worse, we fail to let it in. The result is that the fright and pain continue to live out of control in us. What is so wrong with wanting to murder your boss (or spouse or anyone)? The commandment says, "Thou shalt not kill," not "Thou shall not *want* to kill." Even "coveting" refers to the seriousness of intent, not the mere awareness of that idea.

Ideas, spontaneous impulses, emotions, are neither good nor bad; they just are, and we have absolutely no control over them. It is our judgments about them that cause the pain, that shame us, that make us feel like bad people. We are fused with a judge from our past.

Society tends to reinforce such judgments. So do well-intentioned admonitions to love, to forgive, to have any manner of wonderful feelings and impulses, as if to have them one need only to throw some sort of spiritual circuit-breaker and we will switch from darkness to light. Real love and forgiveness must be earned; they are the result of knowing and accepting *all* our feelings, experiencing them, anguishing over them, struggling with them, and then moving toward another person as an independent, psychologically separating person. It's quite an order, but you can do it.

However, we must start where we are, and where we are is an amalgam of our human capabilities and limitations plus our personal histories. It is not our fault that we are faulted. This realization is *radical self-acceptance.* Without the intention to love and receive ourselves, *just as we are now,* regardless of what we have thought and done in the past, and regardless of what we will think or do in the future, we will always be guarded. We will stay fused. We will not grow out into ourselves.

To observe, to focus clearly on exactly what is happening to us and by us and around us, is a psychologically separated act. When we *seriously take notice*, we are in charge of our life. Even if we experience pain, it is *our* pain. Although we are suffering, we have ourselves. Just noticing our behavior and inner processes interferes with the default tendency to stay fused in the old self-defeating patterns when we operate automatically and unthinkingly. Just by noticing the randomness of our thought processes, the inconsistencies, the irrationalities, the confusion, the pain, and the grief, we reclaim our lives!

That awareness in itself activates spirit, our inner thrust to grow. We begin ever so subtly to move in the direction of self-regard. Changes begin immediately just by the determination to notice our lives. It is amazing. We begin to discover that we have unwittingly turned our lives and destinies over to the forces of fusion and have been unaware of it!

If a person were to spend a year doing nothing more in the way of changing himself than simply observing himself, his behavior and feelings and thought processes, his relations with loved ones, peers, authorities, and those who rely on him, he would grow out into himself by that observation alone. And he might notice some very interesting things about the part mother continues to play in his life.

A sixty-three-year-old man once told me that he knew himself better than anyone else did. I told him that was true in certain ways, but in others it was not. He certainly didn't know about all the wonderful characteristics that endeared him to his many friends and the beneficiaries of his generosity, spiritual as well as material. What he did know better than anyone else was what his *mother* thought about him (or what he thought his mother thought about him). Long gone, she operated in him constantly, evaluating his mistakes and influencing his attitude toward his relationships, particularly with his wife and children. And this is true for most of us as well. What we know best is our mother's appraisal of us, past and present. It is inevitable. We have spent those "hundreds" of years observing and listening and learning how to please her and avoiding her displeasure. How could it be otherwise?

As you practice your newfound mode of observation, try to notice even how your self-centeredness operates. *This* is hard to see. The prospect of surrendering some of our self-centered connection to mother is so terrifying—we believe that we cannot survive without it—that we passionately resist seeing it. We believe we must "know it all" to know anything. We believe we must "control" the world to be safe. We must be approved of and noticed all the time to be worthwhile. But real safety and the overcoming of fear are ours only to the extent that we are able to *surrender* to the universe, to trust the benevolent workings of a power greater than our self. You don't even have to believe in this. If you observe with an open mind, you will realize it to be true. Observe. Sit on the beach.

If, in consultation with your higher power, you form certain clear but flexible *intentions* about your life, and if you let in the strength that comes from merely *observing* as honestly as you can just what your inner processes and behaviors are, and, most important, if you are determined to *radically accept yourself*, much of what ails you will just begin to disappear over time in the normal occurrences of life. There will be a shifting deep inside you, a releasing of your spirit. This change will surprise you. It will seem to occur "behind your back."

However you have stayed enmeshed, it is in accordance with your human nature. Just realize this and the healing will begin.

And this does not mean damaging your friendship with your mother. It means beginning to disentangle the strangling entanglements that have occurred over time, as if you were a fish caught in a net. By disentangling yourself, you will be free—free even to see her as she truly is and to love her as a grown-up loves. She will be free, also, to go her own way. And both of you will be free to grow into the purpose of each of your lives, to return to who you truly are. With separate hearts you will be able to love each other.

4

Breaking the Shame Habit

SHAME TELLS US that what we do is not human. And yet shame itself is the most human of characteristics. Who has not experienced shame?

From time to time there is an outcry that what we humans need is *more* shame. When shock at the outrages of certain people prompts some to condemn them, to shame them, we actually worsen the problem. For shame breeds shame. Shame itself can lead to shameful behavior. Perhaps guilt may help to lessen bad behavior. Certainly the reaction of reality will do that—but not shame. Shame leads to even more shame. Both those who accuse others of shameful deeds and those who are accused feel shame and pass it on. "Shame flows downhill," and *healing* is the only remedy for it and whatever elicited it and whatever it leads to. It can have a value, though, but only between you and you, never between you and anyone else or between anyone else and you. We'll get to that in a moment.

Once I was staying in Sedona prior to attending a conference in Phoenix. I live in a big city with excellent transportation and ordinarily have no need for an automobile. When I travel I rent one, which is a lot of fun—that is, until I need to use any gadgets, because every car I rent has different ones, and I have to learn about them each time. I generally discover this when I go for gas. I fumble around desperately, looking for the tank lid release lever which can be anywhere from right next to the driver's seat to a spot buried deep in the corner recesses of the glove compartment, as I and a crowd of interested onlookers discovered together one sunny morning, a few years back, in South Egremont, Massachusetts.

I am also not so good at pumping gas myself. I often get flustered and have to ask questions of the attendant. This day in Sedona, the young woman who had to direct me was also serving a line of customers in the grocery store and was very impatient with me. I returned to the car feeling humiliated. I managed to get some gas in the tank, and all the while I was preparing my speech to her about how she had been unkind to me and so forth. Fortunately, it took me so long to fill my tank that I had a chance to realize that she had shamed me, and that I was about to return the favor. She could then go on and shame someone else, and I would drive away feeling shamed because of what I had done to her. Therefore, I determined not to shame her, and I went back inside to pay the bill. She was less flustered—I noticed that she was also minding a young child—and she flashed me the most wonderful smile. "Everything go OK?" she asked. I assured her everything had, smiled back, and both of us parted in a friendly mood. The shame habit had been broken for that moment. Ever so many times in the past I had failed to break it; ever so many times I had passed shame on. But in Sedona that day I had not passed it on. There was a little more healing in the world.

I told that story at the beginning of my presentation the next day in Phoenix and what happened was remarkable. The entire audience got excitedly involved, and we had a wonderful hour together. I hardly took notice of the voluminous notes I had prepared. Everyone was fascinated with shame.

We were all psychologists, and yet shame was new to us. Once when I was a patient in psychotherapy my therapist exclaimed, "You have so much guilt!" She didn't realize, nor did I, that what she was referring to was *shame*, not guilt. I had guilt, too, but what I had "so much" of was shame. This was some fifteen years ago, and psychotherapists did not know about shame. There were voices crying in the wilderness like psychologist Helen Block Lewis (*Shame and Guilt in Neurosis*, New York: International Universities Press, 1971), who discovered many of us psychotherapists were not only *not* treating shame correctly, but also, by the nature of some of our confrontations, we were actually creating it in our patients! Another was Alcoholics Anonymous historian Ernest Kurtz (*Shame and Guilt: Characteristics of the Dependency Cycle*, Minneapolis: Hazeldon Press, 1981) who discovered how shame worked when he observed how it was cured in AA meetings. Both of these creative pioneers are only now beginning to be acknowledged.

Shame and guilt are not the same. Guilt is a bad feeling accompanying a deed which violates our own standards of what is right and wrong. It refers to something we have done. Its remedy is to correct the mistake we have made, to acknowledge it to ourselves and the other who is involved, and to make some kind of restitution. Optimally, that should be that. I am suspicious of a guilt that lasts more than twenty-four hours after it has been taken care of. If you have acknowledged your mistake to yourself and the other, and done the best you could to make up for it, you are emotionally and spiritually in the clear. If you are still suffering, something else is going on. It generally has to do with shame.

There is guilt that has to do with feedback to ourselves when we have blinded ourselves to what is good for the universe. In that blindness our moral evaluative mechanism is temporarily disconnected, generally motivated by self-centered willing of some sort. When it comes back on, we are confronted with the discrepancy between our carefully honed sense of what is right and our actions. The "fever" that alerts us to this discrepancy is the painful affect called guilt. And as with fever, it is an important indicator of disease, spiritual dis-ease. Such guilt is our friend. It says nothing about our value as persons. It tells us that we have made a mistake; that we need to do something to remedy the situation. Hopefully, the evaluative mechanism, our conscience, is well tuned: it does not let us off the hook so easily but it does not torture us either. If we are lucky, we have a well-functioning conscience, influenced by our interactions with our parents and the world, but ultimately accepted by ourselves as making sense, now that we have had a chance to look around and observe a little of how the world works.

But there are kinds of guilt that are not so friendly. The first actually appears to be a lack of guilt. Here our evaluation of ourselves is so shaky—the narcissism I have hinted at—that it is virtually impossible to ever acknowledge a mistake. To make any mistake is devastating. So we don't let guilt in, or we deny it to ourselves and others. These are folks who find it impossible to apologize.

At the other end of the spectrum is the person who is riddled with guilt over past mistakes. No amount of forgiveness or reparation will do. The self-flagellation and suffering are relentless. In both instances the root of the suffering lies in fusion with mother. The basic issue is the inability to psychologically separate to the point of making even your conscience your own.

This latter difficulty with guilt is related to shame, for *shame is the anguish at the belief that you are basically, essentially, and irredeemably limited.* It is the conviction that you are flawed, faulted, not *fully human*, and, what is worse, there is nothing you can do about it!

Guilt has to do with doing. Shame has to do with "being." Guilt tells us that we have done something bad. Shame tells us that we have *not* done something, that we *cannot* do something, and because of that we are "worse than" bad. The same behavior can elicit shame as well as guilt if we believe that there is something *wrong* with us for even having made a mistake. Shame tells us that we are *not enough* and that *we have not done enough.*

Shame can be a friend, too. Shame can remind us that we are not living up to our vocation, that we are not fulfilling our calling, that we are not co-creating with the transcendent One in the unique way that we can. The poet who does not write, the lover who does not select a partner, the person whose self-will keeps him separate from forming his will to something greater than himself—all these folks may feel shame. Shame can be a reminder that we are selling ourselves short, that we are not fulfilling our destiny. It is a good reminder. It is good for us to become who we truly are, and shame can be the fever of the soul that draws our attention to our selling ourselves and the universe short. It often has a tinge of sadness with it. Pay attention to this shame. It is healthy guidance. But don't persecute yourself even for this.

Unfortunately, most shame is not good for you. There are two types. One type stems from your having been abused in some form, a psychological shame. The other rises simply from the observation and experience that it is a part of our very nature to be limited, an existential shame. Both types of shame lie to us. They tell us that we are not enough and cause us anguish. The psychological type is the result of having been told in some fashion that whatever we do is not enough. This sets us out on a lifetime quest trying to become enough by doing more and more in a futile attempt to remedy this deep belief. We are enough just because we are alive!

We may have been victims of abuse in a physical or sexual or emotional way. Children tend to take responsibility for this abuse as a way of protecting themselves and their mothers. The result can be a lifetime of fusion and shame. This legacy is profoundly difficult to overcome.

Still others, paradoxically, have experienced shame at their *accomplishments*. Whatever sets us apart from others may threaten us with abandonment, somewhere deep inside us, and unless we are supported and encouraged by parents we may feel shame. These are the folks who are afraid of accomplishment or who "snatch failure out of the jaws of success." It is not commonly understood, but this is a form of shame, too. As you read the paper each day and see the downfall of prominent people, remind yourself that these folks are not evil as much as they are fused and awash in shame and have been long before their present personal tragedy.

These types of shame may be considered "neurotic" in that they stem directly from interactions with our early caretakers and are sustained by our fear of separating from them, both psychologically and emotionally.

The other type of shame that haunts us, the "existential," is because of the very nature of being human and our personal experience and awareness of limitation. This type of shame got us into trouble in the garden of Eden because of our *refusal to accept* that there were some things that we just could not do. Many of us suffer all through life at not being able to accomplish tasks that our egos tell us we should be able to accomplish, and these overweening egos have much to do with our fusion with mother. If we are "one with mother," there should be nothing that we cannot accomplish! We have chronic shame at our "lacks." We "should" be able to do everything. We should be able to make mother happy. We should be able even to overcome death. Our difficulties in accomplishing these impossible tasks result in shame.

It is in the struggle with this shame that our true freedom lies. As we make progress in surrendering the fused notions that are so offended by the reality of our limitations, we will begin to see ourselves as part of something much larger, and at the same time we will be free to pursue our uniqueness. A suggestion of peace and even joy will begin to insinuate itself.

We are riddled with shame. It is part of the human condition to feel shame, both the "neurotic" kind and the "existential" kind. And as was true in my experience in Sedona, we tend to pass it on. If we are inundated with shame—and shame itself makes us feel ashamed—we are often prompted to engage in "shameless" behavior. Much of the behavior we are unhappy with in ourselves is prompted by the experience of the hopeless grip of shame. So shame creates shameful behavior that prompts shaming behavior in others, which leaves both the "shamer" and the "shamee" shamed. One of the most common manifestations of this is *contempt*. We are self-contemptuous due to our perceived "lacks," and we tend to be contemptuous of others as well, seeing *them* as lacking. This is a makeshift way of relieving our own shame, understandable but never really successful, because it gets us into trouble with others and eventually with ourselves. We feel guilty or mean-spirited. We don't like ourselves very much when we are this way.

It is essential that you understand that *there is no way to remove all shame from your life.* It is like a bacterial infection. It will happen; it is human nature. It cannot be avoided. It is one of the limitations of being human, and while this awareness prompts some folks to have even more shame, it can also be the beginning of letting yourself off the hook, of accepting yourself. It is our nature; no one can avoid it. Why feel bad about it?

Recently I participated in a weekend workshop for singers. At the end of the first day each of us had to stand before the others and sing a song we had just learned together. That night we had to prepare a song of our own choosing to perform the following day. If ever there was an activity designed to surface shame, it is singing before others. Standing up there, emotionally naked and unprotected by our strategies of communication, we had to contact the audience from a place inside us over which we had little control. How dare we do this? Who do we think we are? People will see the truth about us. We do not sing well enough. We *are* not good enough. We are awful! Without exception the members of the workshop were overcome with emotion and flooded with shame. Shame is like a cold that never goes away. Some days it is mild; other days it is debilitating. It is chronic, and certain circumstances may always elicit it.

When shame is at its most severe it tells us that we are worthless. It makes us feel that we are subhuman. Not only do we not do enough, *we are not enough*. Not only do we make mistakes, *we are mistakes*. We don't belong on this planet. We are worthless pieces of garbage. But this belief is illusion. *Your joy or your misery in life hinges on getting this one straight.* You are not a mistake. You are innocent!

So: there's the shame that's personal, that challenges us to be all that we can be. This shame can actually be a help. And then there's the shame of our situation in the world, existential shame, the awareness of our essential limitations as human beings. Those limitations are the truth. That's the way it is. When we stop fighting this we can grow out into ourselves, return to who we truly are. Finally, there's the interpersonal shame, the "building into us" of convictions of worthlessness, resulting from the abusive ways in which persons have treated us. I consider as abuse, incidentally, situations where children are allowed to develop the deep belief that they are responsible for the welfare of a caretaker.

Once shame has taken deep hold and becomes part of us, situations can reinforce or trigger it. *Reinforcement* is those situations or persons who continually abuse us even though they weren't the originators of our basic shame. They constantly stir it up and reinforce it. *Triggers* of shame are any persons or situations, some quite innocent, such as my singing workshop, that elicit the shame that is already lying dormant within us. Reinforcers or triggers do not *cause* the shame—it is there already —but constantly stir it up.

It is an unfortunate human tendency that we tend to pass shame on, as if we will get relief from our shame by eliciting the shame of others. When this characteristic becomes chronic we act like perpetual "victims" whose only relief for pain is to launch an attack on others. Someone in the present must be held accountable in order for our shame to disappear. This approach never works; it just perpetuates the problem. It creates self-shaming and very often keeps us from the real issue. For those who shame us today are rarely the causes of our shame, and focusing on them paradoxically "protects" the original source. Sometimes we even have the original source wrong. Chronic unrelieved rage is a symptom of chronic fusion with mother.

45

Constant longing and railing only keeps one firmly ensconced with her. Whether it takes the form of feeling helpless and depressed, of being the angry victim, or of vengefully passing it on by shaming and contempt, *our shame is ours*, and the beginning of its healing is the full acceptance of that. It is our only hope. Otherwise, our entire life will be about shame.

It is crucial that we help ourselves with this human tendency. There can be no consistent joy without breaking the shame habit. We suffer, and we continue to pass it on in our contempt, judgment, and criticism. When enough of us get together in our shame, we pick another group to have contempt for and attack them. And if a whole country or ethnic group organizes their shame in this fashion we have war, for the sake of the "motherland" or the "fatherland." War and prejudice are the institutionalization of shame. And although this is not our fault, the remedy must start with us.

And what is the remedy? Let's go back to our principles of change. First, we must *intend* to break the shame habit, to *consider the possibility* of life with minimal shame, to not be at its mercy. Second, we must *observe, observe, observe*. Don't fight it. Immerse yourself in shame. Feel it, observe it, witness it. *Accept it*, notice the conditions under which it is elicited, notice who prompts it, notice what we say to ourselves at the time, notice our impulse to attack ourselves or to lash back. Notice the tendency to shame ourselves even for feeling shame. Watch it all. Observe, observe, observe. And breathe. *Don't try to change anything.* Employ slow deep breaths.

Accept yourself for having shame. Make it your own. Remind yourself that it is the human condition to feel this. There is no escaping it. Regardless of what anyone says to you or has ever said to you about this, it is perfectly natural to feel shame and to feel it frequently. It is delusion, but it occurs—all the time. The common cold is a form of illness, but it is natural. It happens all the time. Tell yourself that it is OK. Tell yourself that you love yourself. Tell yourself that you are innocent. Accept yourself as a person with shame. It is the human condition. It is the human disability. There is nothing wrong with *you*.

We don't have to let it get the best of us. Take care lest you criticize yourself, alone or in front of others. Sometimes we tend to do this, or we ingratiate ourselves, to ward off the anticipated attacks of others. Just accept the experience when others shame you. And when they begin to treat you well, don't hold their past criticisms of you against them. Remember, they were shamed, too; otherwise they wouldn't do it to you. Let the cycle end with you! And healing will occur "behind your back."

Let your felt shame bring a rededication to radical self-acceptance. Form the intention to love yourself completely, unequivocally, fully, *unconditionally*, without reservation. When shame is triggered—and the trigger may be a success as well as a "failure" or criticism—it has a life of its own. It is like adrenaline pouring into your bloodstream, or a cold which must follow its course regardless of our interventions. Don't take it on directly. Realize that you are powerless over it. The bad feelings, the crazy ideas that will not go away despite every attempt, will just have to exhaust themselves. When you stop fighting, they disappear much quicker. Nature takes care of it. But realize that the bad feelings and the critical ideas are the things that are crazy, not you. What is crazy is the content of the shaming thoughts and the fact that the shame attack is happening at all.

Would that *good* feelings would run through me with such abandon! I woke up feeling wonderful this morning, but there is a good chance that something will happen today that will dash that feeling and summon up my shame. One event in the past can be the occasion of a lifetime of suffering, but good feelings take daily attention. Be aware of this and develop self-loving practices. Be aware that compulsive ideas of shame are delusions about which you can do little directly once they have started. Remind yourself that there is *nothing wrong with you*.

Good feelings are fragile. Enjoy them, but be prepared for shame attacks on them. Don't be discouraged. Be active in the creation of good feelings. Study what makes you feel good and what makes you suffer. Make a "pat yourself on the back" list of the good things you have done, and constantly remind yourself of the loving appreciation of you that your friends have shown. Do it daily. Write it down. It is not our nature to remember these things as it is to remember what is "wrong" with us. We need all the ammunition we can muster to fight shame and its crazy-making ideas and its debilitating emotions. And in the midst of the vicious accusation that shame makes upon you, tell yourself over and over again, "I am innocent." And breathe—slow deep breaths. Notice where the feelings are in your body; accept them. Love yourself.

If you do these things consistently over time and relief comes too slowly, consider the possibility of getting help in the observation of where you are stuck. Find a good psychotherapist, one who is not afraid of the unconscious, who is committed to his own psychological separation, who really listens, who is kind, and who is not afraid of God either. Some folks find meditations helpful. We know little about the biological causes of psychological or spiritual suffering despite what some doctors say. It is tempting to seek magic in a bottle or capsule. But there are side-effects, as well as the possibility that you may be trying to avoid delving deeply into your emotions as I have urged you to do. But keep an open mind about it. First, try speaking to a live person. And never medicate yourself. Go on or off medications only under careful medical supervision.

Shame is isolating. When we are shamed we tend to look down and away. We believe that we are not fit for the company of others. But this is exactly when it is most helpful for us to be with others. A powerful remedy for shame is communication, being with and sharing with others, both formally and informally. Attendance at church, group therapy, membership in clubs (particularly those with a service orientation), athletic events, self-help groups, even concerts—all these remind us of our shared humanity. We are all suffering. Let us be with each other in our suffering whether we speak of it directly or not.

When we suffer, our human tendency is to scramble around for ways of fixing ourselves. We feel shame for having the difficulty and shame for not being able to fix it. Our next step generally is to seek out other humans, such as doctors. This is good. We can do much to help ourselves, particularly if we are open to surrendering to the universe and listening for the instructions of our spirits. Friends, lovers, priests, doctors—all can help us enormously by their wisdom, devotion, and compassion. Don't deprive yourself of any of these helps. But the most profound remedy is spiritual. When we suffer we are painfully aware that we do not possess the power to help ourselves, to make things better. In the next chapter we will consider having a relationship with a *higher* power, one which may provide us with the best hope for banishing shame.

5

From Mom to God

IN OLD SAINT Paul's Church in Baltimore, there is an inscription dated 1692 which succinctly suggests a beautiful philosophy of life. You may have seen it. It is called "Desiderata," that which is to be desired. One line reads, "Therefore be at peace with God, whatever you conceive Him to be."

I do not presume to suggest anything to you about your conception of God, but I am convinced that each of us has one. Only the peculiarities of mother-fusion, a subtlety of self-centeredness, would prompt us to fight this reality. Clearly there is a power greater than ourselves that runs this universe, however mysterious. Go to that beach by yourself for a time and watch. No man-made computer can match what you will experience deeply if you allow yourself.

It is ironic that there is such resistance to the acceptance of this reality, an obstinacy which blindly believes that science knows all or is closing in on all there is to know about the workings of the universe. Some even maintain that it is "childish" to acknowledge such a power. "Mature adults" know that such a belief is not consistent with being independent "realists." Yet none of the great scientists, deeply aware of the profundity and majesty and mystery of the working of the world, denies the notion of a power greater than ourselves. They stand in awe of it. What needs to be understood is not the reality of a higher power but rather those things that interfere with people having some grasp of that reality and coming to grips with it in their own lives.

What stands in the way is fusion with mother.

A higher power is something larger and more powerful than ourselves, the existence of which reminds us that *we* are not all-powerful, and the participation in which provides us with *power*, particularly to do things which we may have not been able to accomplish on our own. So who do you think was our first notion of higher power? Mother, of course. Some of us have a great difficulty throughout our lives in relinquishing, on the deepest of levels, that first belief.

What often is posed as the "adult" position about the higher power is actually a disguised expression of the grandiosity of mother-fusion. For, in reality, the conscious pursuit of a "relationship" with a spiritual transcendent is the only way we can truly, both emotionally and psychologically, separate from mother and fully become who we are destined to be: ourselves. It is the most powerful remedy for shame, as well.

There certainly have been abuses committed by people claiming to speak for this "higher power." Human organizations are fallible, and all material things are corruptible. It is sadly true that much shame has been generated. This is particularly tragic, for the truth is that the intention to formulate your will in accordance with that of the power of the universe will lessen your shame. It will free you to love yourself, unencumbered by the opinion of others, regardless of who they claim to speak for. You will need to please no one. You will just need to be open to the Spirit of the universe as it lives and co-creates in you as the unique, once-in-the-history-of-the-universe person that you are.

What a spot we are in. We are flawed by our self-centeredness. An appeal to a power greater than ourselves can help us move beyond this self-centeredness. However, this very self-centeredness keeps us from making such an appeal. And even when we consciously seek it, the ways we remain fused with mother often interfere with the *development* of our spirituality. What are we to do?

There is actually a lot we can do. If you are forming the intention to separate out into yourself and have been observing, as I suggested, and have been receiving the emotions and thoughts, sometimes crazy or crazy-making, that come up for you, without distracting yourself from them by self-defeating behaviors, then you have been doing a lot. If you have been doing psychological work, perhaps even observing yourself via psychotherapy, then you have been doing a lot. If you have been loving others, perhaps consciously following a spiritual path, then you have been doing a lot.

Psychoanalytic psychology is a step on the long evolutionary journey of humankind to overcome our narcissism. It teaches us something about how this self-centeredness works within us and where it comes from. It has been suggested as a remedy for loosening the grip of self-centeredness. Yes, psychoanalytic psychology is a great moment in our spiritual history. It has taught us about psychological fusion, and it has been brave for doing so, for there is a great resistance to knowing this. We have been talking to each other about it in our scriptures from the beginning. We have been urging each other to overcome it. But we have made little progress over the centuries. We have been stuck.

We must be in the process of psychologically separating in order to be spiritual. We must clear away the blockages of narcissism, the vestiges of childlike connection to mother, to have a grown-up relationship with a higher power. And in the process of doing that, overcoming mother-fusion, that very spirituality will reinforce psychological separation. For no human power alone could loosen the grip on us of our first higher power, she in whose hands our very lives and self and well-being rested for those hundreds of psychological years, and whom we adored.

But our self-centeredness, an expression of the secret pact with mother, may keep us from searching for the transcendent.

And many of us who want to have such a relationship may have it limited by residual mother-fusion. We may sincerely want to be spiritual but we may be stuck and we may suffer, because to be spiritual the spirit must be free, and the only way it gets free is through psychological separation. Without this we are stuck with a child's conception of God, or one that is similar to the one we were taught by mother or "authorities." In fact, we may use such a conception of God as a way of staying fused. God the *Father* and holy *mother* church become symbols for our enmeshment in our own family. True spirituality demands psychological separation, growing out into ourselves, and enduring the suffering that such growing out sometimes entails. The anguish of the mystics speaks eloquently of this. *One has to leave mother to be spiritual.* In this sense, spirituality is psychological separation.

If I am nice to someone, it may be because I feel loving and it spills out toward him, or it may be because I have the conscious intention of acting that way since that is the way I want to be, or I may be trying unconsciously or consciously to get approval of my mother who wanted me to be a "good boy," or it might be a defense mechanism against rage and contempt, an automatic behavior, part of my character armoring. The latter two motivations are psychological, one a defense mechanism, the other an unseparated, fused pattern of behavior. The first two motivations are in the spiritual realm; the first is spiritual in itself, the other might be considered "spiritual practice." There is no way to know this by simply observing the behavior. It is the motivation that is crucial, and a clue to that motivation is the internal state of the actor. Is he at peace? Is he resentful? Does he feel superior or even nothing at all? Does he expect something from the recipient? I'm daily reminded of my spiritual limitations as I hold the door for someone and experience irritation when that person fails to graciously reward me for my "good deed" with an immediate smile or "thank you." Whenever I take the time to reflect on my personal states of disturbance, I will bump into some sort of dependency which insists on a particular response from another. This is my fusion.

The availability to the Spirit is always the result of psychological readiness. Acting on a spiritual "impulse" or pursuing a spiritual end-product is of little avail. The access to spirituality is psychological. The self (which does the psychological work) is at the interface between our ego (the guardian of mother-fusion) and spirit (the developing, moving forward participation in the life force, the transcendent). It is at this crossroads that the decision, conscious or unconscious, is made to become available to spirit. Intention is crucial at this moment and can be "shored up" by spiritual practice, prayer, and meditation. In fact, prayer is the most powerful form of "intention." But without the "decision" or at least goodhearted willingness, the practice itself may be frustrating, the "dark night of the soul." Or these spiritual tools may be used in a self-centered or avaricious way, a sort of spiritual materialism.

I remember a session with a young man named Warren. After some time in therapy, he began to notice what he referred to as "amazing" changes in himself. He was more interested in the world; he felt better about himself; he was happier. We spoke of these changes and his apparent desire to do things differently, to see the world as it really is rather than through the tunnel vision of the past. It seemed as if he were letting go of something. Warren had been obsessed with hatred of his father, and I suggested that perhaps this is what he was letting go. He considered this.

Later in this session he told me he wanted to visit a person in his firm who had been given notice of termination and who, as a result, was being shunned by his fellow employees. Warren wanted to show support for this man. "Why are people being shunned?" he asked. "Why are you *not* shunning him?" I replied. In this regard he mentioned those who helped the Jews in captivity and those who didn't, and the files of the Stasi, the former East German secret police, which revealed how widespread betrayal is even among loved ones. Warren's increasing psychological separation was prompting him to see the world differently. He spontaneously wanted to do the right thing.

Spirituality refers to the extent the spirit is free to follow its natural course, and it spontaneously expands as consciousness does. Before we are free to be spiritual we must diminish the blockages to contacting God, however we conceive him to be. *Psychological fusion must be overcome before spirituality can prevail.*

The great commandment is: "Thou shalt love thy God with thy whole heart and thy whole soul and thy whole mind, and thou shalt love thy neighbor as thyself." In order to love God with your whole heart and soul and mind, you have to let go of mother. You must relinquish her as your higher power. Only then are you free to truly love your neighbor, and, just as important, to *love yourself.*

But there is another side to all of this. Although psychology is a great help, indeed a necessity, it suffers from its own narcissism. Human psychology is stuck in the belief that we can figure out *all* things for ourselves and can solve *all* problems by ourselves. This is its tragic fault. Psychoanalytic psychology is a crucial step along the road to freedom, but by itself the searching person can never take the final step beyond his narcissism and shame and envy. As far as he may have bravely come, he winds up stuck in a dark nihilism when his "independence" ultimately fails to provide him with serenity.

So just as psychological growth is a necessity for spiritual growth to go as far as it can, so, too, spiritual growth is a necessity for psychological growth to go as far as it can. This is not as ironic as it may seem, for the psychological and the spiritual have been intertwined from the beginning. The first psychological texts are the scriptures. Psychology has been a part of spirituality all along, even before philosophy, and later science, snatched it up.

The spiritual imperative is to *surrender*—to surrender to the mystery and surrender to the sacred. Paradoxically, this surrender is the opening to new and more profound realms of reality. If we reject this basic human task, part of us dries up and atrophies. When we have transcended mother, we are on the threshold of transcending reality as we have previously known it. But the narcissism of psychology resists this; it tells us that we can know it all by ourselves, by our wills, and that all there is consists of that which our human vision can provide for us. It denies our essential limitation. It places us directly back in the quandary of the garden of Eden.

But when we make the conscious intention to surrender our wills to a higher power, we stumble upon a new reality, a transcendent reality, an infinitely unfolding reality. It seems like hocus pocus when we try to explain the events that we are now free to be aware of, and our capacity to accomplish things that have been absolutely impossible before. It is actually no more than our entry into an ever-widening sphere of what is real and natural, one that has been clogged by the narrowness of our fusion-vision. When we both psychologically separate *and* surrender to the *magnum mysterium*, the great mystery, we are inundated with aspects of reality to which our self-centeredness blinded us. There is nothing superstitious about this. It is just *more reality* than we are used to! Relationship with the transcendent takes us far beyond what we have previously known and experienced. It is the tragic-comedy of our hubris that we would prefer a more limited vision of reality, but one that we could understand and control, over the magnificence of infinity and its possibility, one which would provide so much more for us, but over which we would not reign!

The various approaches to the transcendent, and their institutions with all their limitations, represent humankind's desire to live in the sacred and make whatever contact we can with the great mystery. And from the very beginning it was experienced that things could be accomplished in one's life by such contact, even though the explanation of these events could only be made in the language and reality of the age, which may look simple and even dumb to us now (I wonder what they'll think of us a few centuries down the road). But it was also in the gatherings of these seekers that compassion for others was encouraged and preached, the compassion so desperately needed to offset the violence of our unseparated emotions, the self-protectiveness of tribalism with its roots in mother-fusion, which horrify us even to this day. Love and compassion were taught as the antidote to self-centeredness and envy. Generosity would replace avariciousness. Shame was banished in the realization and acknowledgment of the inevitability of our essential limitations. We accepted that *we* were not God.

Psychology teaches us that we are not responsible for the reactions of others. But spirituality teaches us that we need to be mindful of the *sensibilities* of others. It teaches us to see our neighbors as fellow sufferers, not as aggressors or opportunists, but with compassion. Psychologically separated from the caretakers of our childhood, we can see our oneness with all our brothers and sisters, including our parents. Whatever our beliefs or our assertions, the truth of our spirituality is in the love of our neighbor.

What good news it is that our spirituality, made possible by the readiness of our psychological separation, winds up being the cure for both shame and narcissism, each side of the coin of fusion with mother—and for envy, too, as we deeply realize that we are enough in who we are.

Spirituality is marked by generosity and the dedication to usefulness to others.

Bill Wilson, the cofounder of AA, wrote in the final pages of his essays on the twelve steps (*Twelve Steps and Twelve Traditions*, A.A. Grapevine, 1952, pp. 124-125, 1986 edition): "*True* ambition is the *deep* desire to live *usefully* and walk *humbly* under the grace of God" (emphasis mine). In this statement he discovers again the deepest, laser-sharp clarity of spiritual wisdom, as did St. Francis when he taught that "it is in giving that we receive."

Giving, generosity, service, and usefulness alone can stand up to the two eternal human bêtes noires: self-centeredness and shame. *Generosity* is both the hallmark of psychological separation *and* the very spiritual quality that cures us of the final bite of fusion.

These spiritual urges, freed by psychological separation, are the muscle and gristle of *love*. In each conscious encounter with the demons of self-centeredness and shame, these spiritual clarities are always victorious.

Finally, as the great commandment reminds us, you are free to love yourself. No longer imprisoned by shame and self-centeredness, you can experience yourself as God does, you can love yourself without reservation. As we leave oneness with mother, we move toward oneness with God and ourselves. We replace mother with a higher power. We can then replace the need for approval by mother and mother surrogates with love of ourselves. We will have radical self-acceptance, and not the grandiosity of "mother-elect" with its constant vulnerability to shame and its constant seeking of justification by fellow human beings. We will approach total freedom from the evaluations of others. For radical self-acceptance *is* spirituality. And wisdom is seeing the world through your *own* eyes, your unique vision, and co-creating with the transcendent.

6

Intimacy among Friends and Lovers

IT IS ONE of those delightful oddities of nature that brings human females and males together at just the moment of psychological necessity.

You know, the snout left the air-bereft tidal basin ponds some millions of years ago, gasping for air and consequently learned to walk, and stood, and here we are.

The dog lopes through the woods this spring and its odor tempts a tick from its tree branch and it wafts gently down to rest on the haunches of the mutt. Ah, love is born, or perhaps friendship, or at least fusion.

Boys and girls tear themselves from their families, their mothers, in the cauldron of sexuality, just at the moment they are capable of the peculiar human capacity called *transference* by psychologists.

Transference causes us to create our families anew in our current friendships, and when it rears its head in a romantic relationship, it is an ironic opportunity to re-experience old conflicts, to release old fusions, to finish the unfinished parts of our personalities, to grow out into ourselves. What a miracle!

Wresting our spirits from our caretakers, bringing to a close the most passionate and loving of all relationships, is our sad and daunting task. Joyfully, to the extent we have had some success at this, we become ready to be deeply related to others. And just as psychology and spirituality reinforce each other, it is precisely our relatedness to others that helps us separate ourselves out even more into our true selves.

From the moment of birth we have manifested a fierce determination to be independent, to articulate our unique selves, to be free. And from that very same moment another part of us had determined to hold on—to hold on to mother, to hold on tight. One inexorable force, our spirit, has kept us moving onward and forward, reaching out and looking out, to taste, to smell, to touch, to *know*. With no concept of this, each of us intuitively united ourselves with the spirit, the power and force of the universe which is life and whose main instrument is love. Although it often passes for love, psychological fusion is the antithesis of life and love. It is stasis; it leads toward death of the spirit. It is an aberration of nature, something that twists and distorts the optimal growing out of loving things.

Love, on the other hand, seeks union, not fusion. It is taking our central-to-self persons and joining in unity, not blending or merging that unique self in fusion. Each of us lives each day in this struggle between spirit and fusion, between growing out and death. It is nobody's fault. It is the human condition. Have compassion.

Our *intention* to grow out into ourselves, our willingness to *observe* our inner and outer processes, to endure what needs to be felt, our determination to pursue *radical self-acceptance*, and, most important, our reaching out to a power higher than ourselves, to provide each of our spirits with the strength to be ourselves and to do what we are called to do—to love. Thus arises a new opportunity to transcend fusion and grow out into ourselves. Our loving relationships are not only fun and joyous, but they are also a healing. This is why we pursue them with such fervor. For loving another has an important psychological purpose. It makes us capable of having another "matter." It allows us to experience the poignancy of another's life. And this person, over time, must grow "to matter," even more than mother herself.

Such a relationship involves two dimensions, *intimacy* and *relatedness*. Intimacy refers to those things "most within" us, and mental contents most sacred to the self. It refers to those ideas and feelings, attitudes and beliefs, fears and hopes, and even the very modes of perception and processing of information that are "most within us." Relatedness is that dimension of interaction that involves the *revelation* of those intimacies. With some people, for example, we are extremely guarded; with others we are more open and revealing. With our lover or life partner, we should be willing to communicate what is most within us, but even here, sometimes especially here, we can get stuck. Relatedness means revealing one's innermost self to another, and this can be terrifying.

We are all so filled with shame. We all fear that to be known will result in rejection. We have been taught that to reveal one's innermost self to another is betrayal of the family. It is very hard for us to do. Yet we must if a loving relationship is to be successful. And this is also the way we grow out into ourselves. For no agent of change is more powerful than a committed, monogamous relationship in which the partners share their intimacies with each other in relatedness. We come together not merely to love and procreate, but to grow! And this is made possible by the good fortune of our impulse to mate, occurring at exactly the same time as the exquisitely human capacity of re-creating our past, *transference*, becoming full blown. Both occur when we leave home.

When we meet and fall in love and desire to be intimate with each other, when the terrible urges to do this far outweigh our shyness and the hiddenness and shame, it is an opportunity for us to learn just where we are stuck as persons, now that the dust of our childhood has settled. And if we stay with each other for any amount of time we shall indeed be confronted with this opportunity. For in the intimate friendship of monogamous devotion, all the distortions and manifestations of our fusion, all the ways we tend to stop seeing the other as he or she is, and instead re-create him or her in the image and likeness of the past characters of our lives, will be abundantly available to our scrutiny. It is in the study and negotiation of these "regressions" that the relationship will stand or fall, and the stretch into new places of psychological separation will be accomplished, *or not,* for each of us.

In this commitment, the forces of psychological separation encourage us to reveal our "intimus," that which is most sacred and special to us, to another. The forces of fusion compel us to stay the same, closed within the original family that we carry around within us. Something must give, and give it does. A battle ensues. Each regresses to early ways of behaving. We unpack our hidden expectations and demands and complaints, and as unsettling as this is (the honeymoon is over), what occurs is the opportunity to finish the unfinished aspects of our personalities. If we are honest and sincere and of goodwill, we grow and change and psychologically separate. In the process we become more of who we truly are, unburdened by the ways we accumulated over the years to stay fused. What is left is truly us!

It is not inevitable that this happens. The couple may "seal over" and cease to be related; they may covertly agree not to be open with each other and manage to continue to carry out their respective fused agendas (sometimes these folks look like "perfect couples" to the outsider). Or they may leave each other, setting off to further chase the illusion that a good marriage is one in which they will never grow at all. But a good relationship is precisely one in which we have to change—not because it is the price we have to pay, as many believe, but rather because it is our biological and psychological and spiritual destiny to do just that. In the good fortune of bumping into a mate as eager as you to know and to be known, an intimacy will develop that will be the most powerful agency of personal transformation in your life.

Marriage and family are a powerful crucible of psychological separation. We must constantly be growing in order to leave our parents. We must constantly be growing in order to let our children leave us. Changes occur in families, insistently and relentlessly, like water rushing to the sea, unstoppable and enormously powerful. And despite the pain and difficulty and troubles in relationships and families, throughout the world love is fired and formed there. Great feats of heroism occur daily and go unnoticed. There is no more beautiful thing than the lifetime growth of two people in love.

But this seems somewhat rare. The divorce rate is still about fifty percent. Many of the rest eventually settle for what Thoreau calls, "lives of quiet desperation." What anguish there is in the lives of two people who have signed up with each other but have no intention of psychologically separating into themselves! What turmoil and despair mark the years of those who continue to demand that the other change rather than surrender to their own growth. What sadness that this, the finest of opportunities to disentangle oneself from our earliest caretakers, to rise up from enmeshment, to leave mother to become the one, unique person who each of us is and history will ever see, will be sacrificed in the service of living out our lives in secret pacts with "mommy," pacts of which we are often largely unaware.

Truly intimate relatedness is characterized by *presence*. Each member of the couple "shows up" for the other most of the time, and does it while continuing to be central-to-self. Being on the wisdom path, they determine to see the world through their own eyes. In the process of overcoming self-centeredness and shame, both show their caring. *Presence is the state of readiness to relate.* It consists of a willingness to come in touch with one's own inner experience (intimus) and make that available to the inner experience of the other. It is very brave.

The opposite of this is *isolation,* the withdrawal into narcissistic fusion. Emotional isolation is the withdrawing of presence (intimacy and relatedness). It really is a regression into fusion with mother, an emotional home-sickness. It does not necessarily mean being alone, away from people. One can be alone and *present to self,* and one can be with others and *in transference,* not seeing and relating to them as they actually are. What characterizes emotional isolation is *avoiding being with self or others in "presence."* It is living in a nostalgic past. The antidote to such isolation is *emotional communication.*

Emotional communication is being genuine with yourself and with each other. It means knowing what you think and feel and communicating it clearly and directly with no manipulative overtones. It is speaking from your innermost being. Emotional communication is being "up front," particularly with your emotions and feelings. It is avoiding any inclination to attack or criticize. It is being open and available to being seen and known. It is revealing your innermost self to your friend. It is a gentle and touching honesty.

Just as important, emotional communication means listening to your partner. It means opening yourself not only to the feelings you wish to communicate but also to the feelings you experience in receiving your partner's feelings in return. It is truly listening, letting the other finish, not formulating the answer, but rather listening to one's own spirit prior to responding. It is being aware of one's own feelings and taking time before responding.

True emotional communication is wanting to know the other, wanting to *receive* the other without trying to change the other. It is not demanding. It is not needing. It is the relative freedom from the need for approval. *It is caring for the other and what happens to the other, yet not feeling responsible for the other. At the same time it is being attentive to the other's sensibilities.* It is making contact with the other being by a psychologically separating human being who can love, not merely fuse.

Lisa's mom, who wrote to "Dear Abby," was upset because her daughter was mad at her. If she were more emotionally independent she might have carefully studied all her feelings and then communicated something like this to Lisa:

Lisa, I hear you when you tell me that you are upset because you were not invited to the wedding, and I understand and accept your feelings. I am delighted to be going, however, and do not accept your notion that I should not do what would make me feel happy because you would not feel happy if I did. One does not have anything to do with the other. I am going to the wedding (I'll bring you back a piece of the cake) and I hope you will be happy for my happiness. If not, that is your choice and I will live with it. If you threaten to punish me for doing what I think is best for me, then I will be angry at you because you would be abusing me. If you threaten to leave me for doing what I believe is best for me, I will be very upset, sad, and frightened. I hope I will be a little angry too. But I will live with whatever feelings are elicited by what I consider to be your hostile and menacing behavior. I will survive, and as a consequence of "feeling my way through," I will grow. For as much as I love you, it would not be love if I neglected doing what is right for me because you didn't approve. We would be fused with each other and it would continue to stifle both of our lives and emotional growth. I am growing by this disagreement, old as I am, and I wish the same for you!

Lisa's mom would be *present*. In the process of overcoming self-centeredness and shame, she is a central-to-self person, willing to feel all her feelings, on the wisdom path, still in the process of articulating herself from her own mother, so that she needn't "transfer" onto her daughter the resolved dependencies of her past. She is growing out into herself, and she makes it possible for her daughter Lisa to do the same, if Lisa is willing to grab the opportunity. Mom has overcome the transference and is able to truly love Lisa, for love *is* the overcoming of transference. She has made *contact* and has replaced *fused* communication with *related* communication.

Psychological separation is being "central-to-self" rather than "central-to-other." This commitment to oneself is sorely tested when one falls in love. We may have left home and become, in some sense, central-to-self, but often we have been in waiting for the "right" person to come along to make central-to-ourselves. We will then "live happily ever after," each feeling responsible for the other. We will set up parallel mother-child relationships with each other to replace the one we "left." This is our unfortunate tendency as humans. The collective expression of this new fusion is everywhere in our culture, even in the marriage ceremony itself. In some deep and unspoken place I suspect the unconscious urge to merge with mother once again is touched among the congregation. The marriage vows are seen as an encouragement to fuse, and it is made with the silent blessing of all in attendance. Perhaps this time it will work. Two will indeed become one and live happily ever after.

Perhaps this time it *will* work but not because two have become one. Each must fight this injunction in order for it to have a chance.

There is a powerful longing to see an "essential" connection between ourselves and the other. I feel this way "because" of you. You "made" me feel this way. In truth, the only essential connection that has ever existed for any of us is that which existed between mother and ourselves in infancy and before. All other impulses in that direction are the deep memory of that bliss which a part of us always seeks to regain.

It is, perhaps, a "sad" reality that any particular feeling we have is the *sole* responsibility of ourselves, but it is so. No one "makes" us feel anything. We choose to respond to another in one of many ways available to each of us at any moment. No particular response is inevitable. Even our love for another is more attributable to our capacity for loving, rather than whatever "compelling" traits the object of our affections happens to have or with which we endow him or her. To love another simply means that we have arrived at the point in our development where we become *capable of loving*.

We take this ability to love for granted. We assume everyone has it. But it is the person who has been on the wisdom path, and who is struggling to leave mother, who is able to love. Many of us are ready for fusion, but only those with the intention to grow out into themselves are ready for love. Then we are willing to love others exactly as they are. We will accept them and not try to change them. We will view conflict as opportunities to finish the unfinished aspects of ourselves.

There is no war between the sexes, incidentally, only people who *live in fusion* and are not free to *let someone else into their lives in intimacy*. Those who are not present to a relationship either because of emotional absence or the extremes of dependence are not free. They often substitute power for intimacy and develop strategies to be "one-up," to have control over the other. If, in the struggle that ensues when one is involved in seeking a position of power over the other, the power seeker does not yield this character defect, the other must leave. If the other doesn't, then that person too is interested in power.

In any dysfunctional relationship, both parties are playing out their own strategies, their own long-learned ways of staying fused with each. And the "victim" is sometimes not too innocent. Twenty years ago, Joel Steinberg was convicted of first degree manslaughter for causing the death of his young daughter. Harvard child psychiatrist Robert Coles examined the role of Steinberg's wife, Hedda Nussbaum, thought merely to be another victim in this horrifying family arrangement. Coles pointed out that the person playing the masochist role is not merely a victim. In studying the case, he characterized "the masochist" (Nussbaum) as "a sly, insistent, clinging aggressor, feeding off and provoking constantly a tormentor's rage." It is natural to take sides in such situations, but in any dysfunctional relationship both parties are scrambling for power, each over the other. The "co-dependent" person needs to be indispensable, the exclusive source of essential gratification to the partner, in order to feel safe. The addict needs to be "sick" in order to be loved. Both life strategies are rooted in an infantile longing for mother, and both result in controlling, "enabling" the pathology of the other, acting out, victimization, blame, and, tragically, even death. The Steinberg tragedy is an extreme example, but much milder variations of this occur daily.

However, there are those on the separation path who are intent on being central-to-self and looking for another who is not interested in fusion but in the fresh loving of two independent people. Their differences, especially those of gender, are relished and enjoyed. They are in no way serious obstacles to intimacy. Those very differences provide great joy.

Such folks generally have other friends, too, *and it is crucial that they do.* They enjoy love of all types and know that the intimate, monogamous relationship is just an instance, a very special instance, of friendship in general, and that no one relationship can satisfy all the emotional and spiritual needs of anyone. It is good, too, that such lovers have friends because even in the most psychologically separated among us there is still the powerful pull toward enmeshment, *especially* once sexual intimacy is initiated. Other friendships serve as a sort of check on that tendency. In a good relationship, each supports and encourages the other in their friendships. If one member of the couple or both do not have good friends, they are not only limiting their own potentialities to grow out into themselves, but they are also putting their very intimacy with each other at risk.

Growing out into yourself involves emotionally leaving the family you came from, and even that which you created. It means being able and willing to experience being totally alone—one with yourself in the world—while simultaneously being emotionally merged with all living things that are, ever were, and ever will be.

Does this mean we cannot have loving relations with our parents and siblings and children and lovers and friends and acquaintances? Just the opposite. In the inner atmosphere of the truly psychologically separating spirit, it is for the first time actually *possible* to have *genuine* relatedness. We acknowledge that we are all fellow strugglers and we can love, support, and celebrate each other. Because each relationship has its unique characteristics, each is like a fingerprint. And those we have blood with, those we have years with, those we have special physical, psychological, and spiritual relatedness with, etch our souls. They actually help us separate—define our selfness. We need each other to become ourselves.

But it is love with a stranger that first provides the possibilities to confront the unfinished aspects of our personalities and to yield the old ways to make way for a return to who we are. An exclusive, long-term committed relationship demands this of us, and as such it is a gift. Our other friendships are powerful supports and do the same, but to a lesser degree. Intimacy and relatedness clear the way for us to open our hearts in love.

It is sad to give up our old fused ways, but it is also exhilarating, because to be a live, psychologically separating human is thrilling. We give up our childishness, our avaricious needs to have people re-create old roles. We accept our life, our existence. We appreciate the absolutely unspeakable gift of being alive, and our payment for that gift is to be alive and to pass it on.

We love, we lose our lovers, we pick ourselves up, dust ourselves off, vow we'll never love again, and then we do, if we are lucky. For we are lovers, we humans, and the most poignant thing about us is that, in spite of it all, we try again; we reach out across the chasm of our essential aloneness to bridge it with our love, and we often do. With all our limitations, human love and human friendship are the greatest things about us. And when we have found it, if only for a moment, it is the best there is.

7

Loving Yourself Madly

YOU HAVE FORGOTTEN how wonderful you are. Picture an eighteen-month-old toddler dancing happily, surrounded by beaming adults. You were that child at one time, unencumbered by memory, with no history of yourself either for yourself or for others. You were sheer joy at that moment, and when that joy would be dissolved, it would be by an event of the present, not by a message to yourself. You were wonderful that day; everyone knew you were wonderful. Even you knew that you were wonderful. And you are just as wonderful now. You have just forgotten, that's all. Things have happened; opinions have been formed; philosophies have been forged; deep beliefs have arisen. But underneath all of that, you are as wonderful as you were that day.

You are the perfect you the way you are. Even if you are suffering beyond belief this very moment, it is not because you are not the perfect you. There is nothing wrong with *you*. You may wish to get relief from your suffering. You may form the intention to do so; you may observe yourself and life and your own life, by yourself or with a helper; you may strive toward radical self-acceptance. By doing these you will lighten the pain. It will take some time to loosen the blockages to the spirit, but it will happen, and when it does you will not be any more perfect than you are now; you will just suffer less.

Psychological separation, growing out into yourself, is *separating*, not arriving at any clearly describable place. It is a

70

process, a dedication. The most humble of us who takes a tiny step toward self may be more courageous and accomplished than the very gifted person who does great things without much effort. There is no measuring these things. The only arbiter is you, your honest encounter with yourself. All that is needed to be on the wisdom path is *intention, observation, and radical self-acceptance*. The result will be a life beyond your wildest dreams but not one that we can envision or strive for ahead of time. We must leave that to the transcendent nature of things. But this is not a reality that pleases our ego. Many of us would prefer growing less and suffering more so long as our ego can take the credit. Merely to form the intention, observe, and radically accept ourselves, and receive graciously what the universe provides as a result, is ego deflating, even if what we get is far beyond what our limited selves could have accomplished by our egos and wills alone.

I attended a reunion of my men's peer group recently. I have not been a member for four years, but I knew all of the eight men who showed up. Four were still active members. At one point I suggested that we share what we have learned about life since the last time we were all together. A lively discussion ensued. When it came my turn, I told them that I had discovered that radical self-acceptance is my most important task for the rest of my life, and that I was determined to go about it with vigor and determination. I had many plans, many projects I wanted to accomplish, many people I wanted to love more and better, but first and foremost was my determination to search relentlessly for ways of re-experiencing the truth of my innocence, to feel the joy that is the human equivalent of looking like a beautiful flower or a sunset. Like my friends in the group and like you, I have suffered a great deal in this lifetime and I wanted to reduce my suffering. I wanted to remove, as much possible, that part of my suffering which came from the old fused notions and habits.

Two of the members started an abstract conversation about "why" people did not accept themselves. Then a third said that he did not think it a good idea to accept oneself so readily. "Ten years ago I was a mean and selfish person. If I had accepted myself then, I wouldn't have changed and the people who are in my life now might not be. You have to be careful about accepting yourself. How would you change for the better?" Most of the others seemed to agree. They began speaking of the "monsters" of the world—Hitler, Stalin, the person who blew up the federal building in Oklahoma City. "Should these persons radically accept themselves?" "It's OK if the good people do, but what about the bad ones?"

"Do you really think the mayhem and murder and cruelty going on all around us in this city this very moment is being done by people who *love* themselves too much, who *accept* themselves too much?" I replied heatedly. Everyone ignored me. The discussion continued about just who should accept themselves and who shouldn't. There was considerable passion. Finally, I interrupted: "You're all afraid that if you completely accepted yourself you would have to look at where you don't love yourself, and if you did that there would be the danger of leaving your mother!" No one seemed to hear this either as the discussion about making sure the bad guys didn't love themselves continued. Why are we so afraid of loving ourselves?

In between "insight" (of psychoanalysis) and "self-determination" (of cognitive or will therapies) lies the "I," the self, *which must be nurtured by acceptance* in order to take responsibility for itself. We tend to avoid this responsibility by endless intellectual insight or repetitive and constantly failing determination, because to realize *the responsibility of the "I"* is to elicit the terror of our underlying fusion-based fear: I will not be able to take care of myself and I will die. Radical self-acceptance is the primary autonomous act. It is a profound separation step. It implies that we are *enough* by ourselves. We no longer are little boys and girls trying hard to become "better" in order to please mom.

Radical self-acceptance is receiving oneself willingly and completely. It means that we completely accept as ourselves *any* particular characteristic or behavior or feeling. Does this mean that we never wish to change something? Not necessarily. However, the desire to change is not prompted by self-hate, self-criticism, self-loathing, guilt, or shame. We may have a sense that we are not yet fully who we truly are, and we may wish to move toward that fulfillment. But we are humble in that ambition, realizing the difficulty of relinquishing old ways, understanding that, in some sense, these behaviors have been friends. We also acknowledge that our notion of what would be best for us at a particular moment may be incorrect, or at least limited.

Radical self-acceptance is accepting yourself exactly as you are: receiving yourself with no strings attached. *This is who I am.* You bring no evaluation or judgment to yourself, either positive or negative; you needn't do anything except to take yourself in and enjoy your experience of being alive—just noticing, observing, and, in as neutral a way as possible, *receiving* yourself exactly as you are in this moment with no caveats or conditions. "Learn from the way the wild flowers grow. They do not work or spin. But I tell you that not even Solomon in all his splendor was clothed like one of them" (Mt 28:29).

Is this not freedom? Relief? This is *release* from all our demons and *is more important than change itself.* Radical self-acceptance is *ceasing to aspire toward anything;* we move in the direction of joy. *To give up self-evaluation is psychological separation.* We are what we are; what is of necessity is, and that is to be one with the transcendent. Love of self and others is the celebration of *what is* with *no desire to change it.* As soon as you want to change it, it is less love. Love is *knowing* without trying to change, knowing the other *just as is,* not a mixture of "as is" and "as I want you to be." Self-acceptance is the same. And lo and behold, just as we lose interest in change, it often occurs "behind our backs."

In group therapy one night we batted about this question: Is it possible to have nothing about us—present behavior, memories of the past, thoughts of the future—elicit suffering and shame? Everybody became disoriented. It is hard even to think of these things. It is hard because such a state of existence implies psychological separation. When we have separated from mother, we are free to accept and approve of ourselves, free to approve *just because we decide to*, not because we meet any standard. We no longer need parental approval. We no longer need the approval of anyone. We are free. We can then release ourselves from the agendas of the past and choose the new in our lives as we come upon it.

The reason that we experience joy in spiritual events, or in a new love, or the birth of a baby, is that these release us, for the moment, from the chronic sense of unworthiness that each of us carries within. This release seems possible for us with a guru, or fellow seekers, or in the presence of new life, or a beloved. But to release unworthiness *by oneself*, alone—that is the challenge. This is more than *replacing* a fierce and critical parental image with a more loving and nurturing one. This is psychological separation, *a decision to know your worth simply as an alive person, a co-creator with the transcendent.* You overcome your resistance to wisdom, see freely what you can see, and, in your own "God-sense," look at yourself and others and joyfully say, "It is good." You give up on the compulsive need to have control over yourself and others. Not only are you not more self-centered and selfish, but you are also actually *more* loving, tolerant, and generous to all living things.

Loving yourself madly is not selfishness. Selfishness is parsimonious; love is expansive. Selfishness is when you think there is not enough and you must hoard everything for yourself. Radical self-acceptance is knowing that you *are* enough, and that there *is* enough. When you love yourself madly you want to give, you want to share. There is no room for selfishness, avariciousness, greed. You love yourself and it spills over onto others. You are generous and giving because you are safe in your self-caring. Selfishness comes from fear. Radical self-acceptance transcends fear. It is joyous, it is expansive, and it is sweetly humble.

The charge of "selfishness" toward someone truly striving to love himself comes from the fused demons within that do not want to see anyone truly psychologically separated. It threatens their secret pact with mom with its hidden grandiosity and its willful ambition to control, its hubris. The deep acceptance of any limitation, our essential humanness, is very hard for us. There is in each of us a grandiose belief that we should have no limitations or parameters at all. We may disguise this by self-criticism, masochism, or whatever, but it is there, an underground standard by which we measure and torture ourselves. We cannot accept ourselves because we refuse to give up this grandiose image. Once again, it is ego, and fusion with mother fuels this delusion. Making peace with life demands continual surrender to reality, acknowledging that we are limited, that we will die, that we are not in perfect control. This last surrender is the hardest—that we are not in perfect control, even over our destinies. It is a dramatic blow to our narcissism.

Actually, we are flawed only when compared to our grandiose expectations of ourselves. We are what we are—merely human. It is when mother-ego distorts what we are that we have troubles, whether you call it psychopathology, hindrances, evil, or sin. The very notion of perfection only comes from our perception of the demands of mother, real or imagined, and the need for her acceptance. Self-acceptance is the ultimate psychological separation, the spiritual act of knowing that you are not God, but that you are just fine in your humanness and "imperfection."

Radical self-acceptance is so torturously difficult for us! To accept ourselves as perfectly OK with all our limitations, relinquishing ego and grandiosity, means leaving mother. And leaving mother means accepting graciously the omnipotence of our transcendent spirit, and even surrendering to death as none of our business. The payoff for this is a life of joy, pleasure, and love, experiencing a fullness and power we did not know was possible. By our gift of surrender to the universe, by our generosity, by our goodwill, we get all life has to offer.

Have as your intention a complete and total acceptance of yourself and everything about you. *Stop trying to change yourself.* Accept yourself as a given. Notice "mistakes" but don't "try" to change them, and *never* make your mistake an excuse for self-abuse. It is human to make mistakes. You are what you are. If you surrender to that, and *sincerely intend to be* what you are supposed to be in the transcendent (as opposed to egoistic) scheme of things, then that is what you will become. Whatever that is, humbly accept it. Remember: self-acceptance *precedes* any change. If change is to occur it must start with loving yourself radically! It is such an irony that we fear that we will not change if we totally accept ourselves. When we love ourselves madly we will not tolerate any behavior in ourselves that will interfere with that love. *For this reason, radical self-acceptance (RSA) is the most powerful agent of change there is!* No real and long-lasting change is possible without it.

When I am disturbed, the essence of my disturbance is what I call "shortness of RSA." Like shortness of breath, I don't have enough life-sustaining self-love. When anything about life disturbs me, it is shortness of RSA. When I demand too much of others because of my dependencies, the disturbance is shortness of RSA and the need to get it from outside myself. When I criticize others, it is shortness of RSA. When I am contemptuous, it is shortness of RSA. Shortness of RSA often comes from shame, and we know that shame often prompts us to humiliate others, whereas RSA expands and tends to envelop others in loving affirmation. Whenever I behave badly, for any reason, or about anything, or with any provocation, it is shortness of RSA. I am not loving myself sufficiently that day.

Just as is true in our struggle with shame, we need to develop strategies to help us love ourselves. Strange as it is, loving ourselves does not seem a natural thing for us humans. Self-centeredness, with its connection to mother-fusion, seems more "natural." The spontaneous love of the toddler appears awkward for us as adults. Each day I am engaged in the struggle between my transcendent-born spirit which wants me to love myself madly and my mother-fusion which wants to keep me dissatisfied with myself, wallowing in an unseparated swamp of trying to better myself to win mommy's approval. If I keep on trying to improve she will be proud of me and I will be safe with her in familiar feelings of malaise, and I will live forever. Or I rebel only to come sheepishly back in search of her approval, real or symbolic.

I need all the help I can get to love myself. I start each day reminding myself that I am not God and asking for help in doing what is right for me to do that day. I sign up with the universe. And I form the intention to love myself. Sometimes, I say, "I love you, Jim." Try that yourself. Tell yourself that you love you, and use your name. How did it feel? Sometimes I have great resistance to saying it to myself, or telling myself, in a personal way, that I love myself. Other times it is easier, though it's generally a little awkward. I have no trouble telling my children or my friends that I love them, but it's a little awkward telling myself. Strange, isn't it? But I do it, like a shy teenager.

Most important, I *form the intention* to love myself that day. I get myself on track. I do all the things I suggested to you when we spoke of "growing out" and "breaking the shame habit." Sometimes I'll discuss my self-accusations with myself when they arrive—and they generally arrive at some time or other—and try to reason with myself. This rarely works. If I am inclined to blame others I pray for them, wishing that they receive all the good things I want for myself. Sometimes I join the self-attacks and make them deliberately worse. I help myself "bottom out," and sometimes I actually feel better because I have stopped fighting. Mostly I *enter deeply* into the feeling, whatever it is, trying not to pay too much attention to the racket in my head, just as I might try to ignore the overly loud bass on my neighbor's stereo. I go about my business. I can always do that no matter what is going on within. And I try not to act out. I try to avoid doing something that my demons desperately want me to do, something that I can regret later, something that will fuel the fire of my self-contempt. I go about my life. I take care of my business.

I've arranged my life so that I have wonderful friends, membership in organizations, and hobbies that give me great joy. I'm blessed with a loving and psychologically separating family. I try to be of service where I can, and I make some effort to keep in shape physically. I work on my spiritual life, particularly mindful of the shortness of my life, and how happy I am to be alive. And over time I feel better about myself. As a result I am more and more happy and eager to pass on what I have learned, as so many others have done for me.

Loving oneself madly, radical self-acceptance, does not so much mean that we always are feeling good, but rather *that we have taken a stand about ourselves.* We become determined to love and accept ourselves *as we are,* and we will receive whatever comes to us about ourselves from that vantage point. To be self-critical, as the Buddhists teach us, is *delusion.* We can be aware of the delusion, stand apart from it somewhat, take a position about it. We need not prove our value to anyone. We need not fight with anyone. But we shall never join our demons by public self-deprecation. We will respect all living things, especially ourselves. Our philosophy will be to feel deeply what we feel, affirm our self-love, and do the dishes when they need doing.

Bad feelings and crazy, self-critical thoughts will pass like a river running to the sea, and our basic love will seep through from under the hatred just as sure as the sun will rise and the tide will come in and there is a wisdom guiding the universe. Our deluded self-centeredness can fool us for just so long. Joy awaits.

Loving yourself is not self-centered, not uncaring, not indifferent to the plight of others. Loving yourself madly, radical self-acceptance, total, unremitting, profoundly deep self-respect is the purpose of life. It only takes two things: the deep intention to do it, and all the courage you can muster.

8

Joy

JUST AS SHAME is what we experience when we believe we are not enough, joy is the emotion we experience when we know we *are* enough, when everything about us is acceptable to us, when we truly know deep down that we are perfect the way we are, although there may be things about us that we or others think need changing.

The naysayers of joy say we shouldn't expect it, or at least extremely rarely. Some feel they can only go after it with drugs or addictions, and they suffer a terrible price. Suffering, sadness, misery, pain, and loss are the human condition, others say. Work, work, work, to improve yourself and you are never done. There is no time for joy.

Joy is our birthright. As with the toddler and its mother and father, joy is the celebration of life. We have the right and the obligation to pursue it full time. We deserve to clearly know the truth that we are wonderful. We are gifts to our parents, and to the universe, just as our children are to us. We are God's partners. Let us rejoice and be glad. Re-JOY!-ce.

We all live in a massive distortion which obscures the reality that each of us deserves the highest of awards *just because we do life*. Consider this: we don't know where we come from, we don't know where we are going, we don't know what our life means. We love, starting with mother, and we have to separate from her and from all our subsequent loves. We know there is a higher power and we reach out in our fog, but we really don't know how to get to him or her—even the sex of this *magnum mysterium* is a human approximation. We know somewhere that we must forge a relationship with ourselves, and if we are lucky we do, though it is very hard. And then we die, and it seems we lose that relationship, too. No matter what we involve ourselves with or how we distract ourselves, these realities linger somewhere inside us. Yet we survive, we endure, we persevere, we pass it on, and, for the most part, we make the best of it. *We are good sports, we humans.* The notion that we should beat up on ourselves *for anything* is preposterous.

Distressingly often when I say these things to people, there is a groundswell of opposition. "If all I do is have fun, how is the world going to function?" "If I don't try to change all my bad habits, I will not be a good person!" The list is endless. And it is the *ferocity* of the rejection of joy that is the amazing thing. True, we must think of our duty; true, we need to spruce ourselves up here and there. But shouldn't the idea of having more joy in our lives cheer us up a *little*? It has that effect on me, though God knows I eke it out by daily combat with my demons. I have come to understand that at the bottom of our joy phobia is the fear of losing mother. For joy is eminently separate. It is the most personal of decisions. To be truly joyous you must be able to stand alone, perhaps propped up sometimes by those on either side of you, but alone in your wisdom, seeing the world with your own eyes in your uniqueness and oneness with the transcendent.

And this uniqueness, this personal vision is purchased by the commitment to psychologically separate, to form the clear and resolute intention to wrest your life, your emotions, your thinking, your acts, to wrest who you truly are, back from your earliest caretakers. We will never feel the frequency of joy of the toddler. Too much has happened to us; we are no longer the *tabula rasa*, blank screens with no memory to haunt us. It is too late for that. But for this much it is not too late: to make the conscious decision to lead our own lives, to search for our vocations as persons. *We can unequivocally commit to being on our own side.*

No matter what madness rushes through our heads and no matter what compulsivities may have us in their grip, no matter how bashed we may be by shame and guilt, no matter how discouraged we may become at our self-centeredness, we can always tell ourselves that we love ourselves. For our suffering is not because of us. It is the human condition, and it is a strange condition, full of mystery. Embrace that truth and forgive yourself. Live each moment, and disregard whatever negative thoughts anyone has about you—*and show yourself.* You owe it to the universe to contribute your specialness. Do not be afraid. We will never be toddlers again, but we *can* have a great time here on earth as grown-ups. We are called to love and receive ourselves fully and have joy as a result.

It is a sad truth that mother cannot save us from death (though most of us still desperately hold onto that notion, generally way below conscious awareness). No one can. Don't throw away your life in the belief that homage to her, or to a surrogate through fused thinking, emotions, or behaviors, will save you. Refusing to forgive yourself, tenaciously holding on to guilt, wallowing in shame or any kind of suffering will get you nowhere. It is a waste of time and of your life except where it gives you information about the world. But loving yourself fully and completely *with absolutely no exceptions*, and deeply desiring to make your life part of the higher wisdom of the universe, will often result in joy, and it will even make possible a happy relationship with your mother, in person or in your mind!

The strategy has been laid out in this book. First and foremost is the willingness to feel whatever it is that you are feeling at the moment. Your emotional state right now, if you stop and identify it, it is like the "subject" in a fugue. If you listen to any fugue or "round," whether it be "Row, row, row your boat" or Bach's *Art of the Fugue*, the first or central theme is the subject. The composer plays with that theme, by repeating it or changing the rhythm or whatever, to make an interesting mosaic of sound. It is like that with our lives. We can break any moment of our lives down into such "subjects." And by observing, you can notice all the things around us that we tend to do in response to that subject.

Speaking of music, I was at a concert the other day, and five minutes before the scheduled beginning the small concert hall was eighty percent empty. My companion and I slid from the side of the row we were in toward the center. Just before the curtain, the place rapidly filled up, and at the exact moment the conductor was taking an introductory bow a couple came in, complaining that we were sitting in one of her seats. There were many good seats around us but she insisted on the one in which I was seated. Her companion graciously moved down one seat but she sat next to me and hectored insistently in my ear, "You are in our seats! *You are in our seats!* YOU ARE IN OUR SEATS!" I quickly moved down a few seats. I was boiling. As in Sedona when I was trying to fill my car with gas, a vitriolic speech formulated itself in my mind. The Brandenburg concerto wafted through the hall as I ruminated about how self-centered she was, how ungracious, how insensitive to my feelings. Who does she think she is anyway? I wanted to glower at her. I wanted to do *something.* I sat in the midst of these intense feelings for a few moments and then determined that I was not going to have this concert be about this woman. I stepped into the feelings, surrounding myself with them, and the anger yielded to a small sadness; suggestions of tears teased my eyes. I recognized the emotion: Shame! She had shamed me, or, more properly, I had reacted with shame to her critical tone. This was the "subject" of this moment of my life. All the ruminating about her, all the other feelings, all my guilt about my anger, all my secondary shame about even having such feelings, were elaborations of this subject of shame. I took a deep breath and it released a little. I got back to the concert. Every once in a while I would think of it again, wince with shame, and have the impulse to do something to her. Then I would smile at myself, and I was at the concert again.

Just before the end of the program I realized the difference between the psychological and spiritual aspects of this little incident. The realization of my shame, my willingness to feel all the feelings I need to feel, including the anger and humiliation, and the consequent release of the preoccupation, were the psychological aspects. I formed the intention to study the problem, to stay immersed in it, and to not escape by some kind of mental gymnastics. I also stayed on my side. No matter what was going on in my mind, even self-critical thoughts, I did not join them. My goal was to feel better and to act well. I owed it to myself. Although I didn't formulate it just this way at the time, in my upset I had jumped back into the "inner atmosphere" of my childhood, which was filled with instances of being shamed for my mistakes or even uniqueness. It has left me, to this day, somewhat shaky and hesitant about public functions. It was the source of my vulnerability to a situation such as this.

Without going through this process that day, I may never have gotten to the point where my spiritual convictions had a chance. I might have acted out in a very unspiritual way and then rationalized my behavior. All sorts of unkindness are justified in the name of "justice." But in my awareness and acceptance of myself (perhaps it was Bach) I was free to let my spiritual principles carry the day. "Psychology" got me to the "wall," so to speak, but spirituality got me through it. I didn't "get even" with her in any of the devious ways I could have concocted (even when she upset the whole row by leaving midway to greet and chat with a friend, and then haul the friend back though the row to sit beside her). I was tested once again after the performance when I found myself behind her in a receiving line for the artists. Despite my psychological process and spiritual awareness, I still had the urge to get even in some way, to shame her back. It was only my relationship with a higher power that protected me (and her). It was neck and neck, but he carried the day and I can write about this now without shame and even have fun.

Stay in your feelings; live in your feelings. When you do you will often feel sadness, because we spend much of our lives mourning. It is our nature. Life is filled with loss. Letting go of mother is just the beginning. Remember, too, that guilt and shame will always be with you. Anything we have ever felt guilty about or places where we are "shame-vulnerable" will always be with us. It is similar to a formerly broken bone being sensitive to weather or to deep touch. Like these physical sensitivities, guilt and shame can "flare up" without our doing anything. Expect it; don't be thrown by it. At the same time, work on your spiritual and emotional hygiene. Loving ourselves is not automatic anymore. It takes determination to maintain our self-love. We need to be vigilant in our behalf—not because we need to improve ourselves, but rather to heal ourselves and keep us sound.

You may have thought I was joking when I suggested earlier that you keep a list of the good that you have done. I was not kidding. It takes one bad deed for a lifetime of misery, but it takes daily focusing to remind you of your lovableness and your worth. It is one of those weird things about us. We all need happiness "prostheses," tricks to remind us of the truth that we are just fine the way we are. Every time we perform an estimable act, it helps us feel good about ourselves, but we need a structure to remind ourselves of them. They tend to evaporate. Record them. You will find this an interesting exercise. You will be amazed at the wealth of responsible and accomplished and loving things you will have done by lunch! But the demons of fusion want to keep you in the dark. You have got to keep reminding yourself to notice. Write it down!

Constant work on your relationship with God, as you conceive him to be, is crucial to joy. The more you sincerely form your intentions to his, the more estimable your behavior will be and the more serenity, forgiveness, and tolerance of self and others will be the hallmark of your life. This is just the way it is. The only real remedy for an overweening ego and its sidekick, shame, is the healing that comes from surrendering to a higher power.

And then there are the practical things. Join groups; there is healing in shared experience. Consult experts; psychotherapists, ministers, spiritual guides. Don't hesitate to use them in your search. We all need help and we need a lot of it—and we need it all the time. Avail yourself of those who have dedicated their lives to help. Just never make any of them your higher power. That would just be turning them into a reincarnation of your mother.

Take care of your health. Separate your notions of good mental, spiritual, and physical health from those who raised you. Make your own decisions. Think them through. We need sound bodies to support us in this journey. Take responsibility for your body. Love it and treat it well.

Become increasingly aware of your natural tendency to fuse and to abandon your uniqueness. Formulate a clear, conscious *intention* to psychologically separate and make your life your own. *Observe your inner experience* and receive it all; don't run away from it. It is the "subject" of your life. Make it yours. Feel all of it. Form the intention to *radically accept yourself.* Never leave yourself, never stop loving yourself, never betray yourself, always stand by your side.

Love others, friends, and/or a life partner. Open yourself to them and receive their attempts to reveal themselves to you as well. Tolerate the "regressions" that occur when there are conflicts between you, and learn from them. Grow out into yourself in these loving contacts.

Always nurture the capacity to be with yourself, by yourself. In solitude we touch our deepest uniqueness and the most profound unity with all of life. After all is said and done, it will be in solitude that you will surrender the grip of mother. In solitude you will cease being one with her and will become one with yourself, one with others, and one with God. So few do this. Be one who does.

And when you get on this path, the wisdom path, your life will be yours. You will walk with yourself. As time goes on you will notice certain things about yourself.

* You will notice that your *thinking,* your *emotions,* and your *acts,* even when routine, will bear your unique stamp. You will be able to think about anything, feel anything, do anything, refuse to do something. It will all be up to you. Your life will be yours. You will be free.

* You will notice that you are becoming independent of the judgment of others. You pay attention to the reactions, attitudes, and feelings of others, but this is for information, not instructions. You become the final arbiter of your behavior. You are not afraid of what others will think of you. You are free.

* You don't feel responsible for others, nor do you expect them to feel responsible for you. You are easily able to say "no" to others, and you can graciously accept their saying "no" to you. You are responsive and empathic to their feelings and go out of your way to be kind and generously cooperative, but you know you are not responsible. At the same time you are quick to acknowledge your imperfections. You have little difficulty in apologizing when you make a mistake or hurt someone's feelings. You are free.

* You find yourself feeling and being very generous with respect to both your time and your material goods. You easily praise people. You are not afraid of running out of anything or becoming depleted. You know you are enough and that the universe is infinite in its abundance. The soul-rotting anguish of envy increasingly dissolves. You are able to celebrate the success and good fortune of others. You just naturally feel "giving" and receive the joy that results from such generosity.

* You find yourself feeling increasingly grateful—grateful for the magnificent gift of life, thankful for the innumerable blessings each of us has, which becomes clearer as we let go of

fusion. When we step out of fusion, the world and its gifts are truly overwhelming. We experience the joy of that awareness and live in an emotional state of appreciation. We are aware of how much so many people have given to us, living and gone, known to us and not, and we are quick to show our appreciation to others. We are thankful for all that our mothers have done for us, most of which we will never even know, and for the sacrifices of our fathers as well. In our generosity, we forgive.

It is coming to the time, dear friends, when I must stop, but I have one more thing to tell. Now that I have suggested all you might do to psychologically separate, be yourself, find God, love and be happy, I must tell you that we all miss by a mile. I jokingly tell folks that it is definitely possible to do it all, but that it takes a minimum of one hundred years of living until the job is completed. So develop a lot of patience and tolerance for yourself and others along the way.

We will feel all there is to feel, and then we won't; we will intend to separate out and to observe and to radically accept ourselves, and then we won't. We will experience shame and steadfastly refuse to pass it on, and then we'll forget. We will be open and honest with others and our lovers, and then we won't. We will be glad for the happiness and good that comes our way, and then we will lose it to envy and jealousy. We will form the intention to participate in the plans of a higher power, and the next moment we'll drop the whole program and rush willy-nilly into headstrong and selfish and self-defeating behavior.

Most of us miss by a mile, all the time. And we'll probably continue to do so. But this much we can always do. We can pick ourselves up, dust ourselves off, affirm that we love ourselves even when we are not inclined to, and resume where we left off. And know we are not alone, nor are we weird. It is our nature.

Perseverance is our strength: chipping away; keeping at it gently but persistently; accepting the accommodations we make in our relationships yet patiently trying to be more giving; and most important, building daily our devotion to loving and accepting ourselves *just as we are at this moment.* No one or no thing can truly prepare us for all that life will demand of us. It seems that as soon as we have one thing pretty well figured out, we are faced with an entirely new stage of life, for which we have no preparation at all. Take it easy on yourself. Have compassion. Oh, and don't forget your sense of humor! I can't claim to know much about the essential characteristics of my higher power, but I am absolutely certain of one thing: he has a joyous and robust sense of humor. I'm sure he's holding his sides in laughter most of the day, and that he wants us to do so too. Better than the wisest counsel from theologians and philosophers and psychologists is a good belly laugh. Go for it! The laughing Buddha is my man.

A few final thoughts about mom. A patient told me that he feels so unfused with his mother these days that he is able to attend to her needs—she is in her eighties—with no resentment. When we disentangle our fusion with mother, it does not mean we reject her. Often, we are able to relate lovingly and generously for the first time. When you cease being enmeshed either in hatred or in overestimation, you are free to see mom as a separate person, and you, as a separate person, can truly love her and forgive her and appreciate her and even be grateful—or at least be just, and at peace about her. When you "let her go," you can relate to her, you can love her. She is your friend, not your higher power. When fear has abated through psychological separation and spiritual growth, the poignancy of our enmeshment with mother can be surrendered to the deep love of special friends. You no longer believe it is *essential to her welfare* for you to be a certain way or to do certain things. You no longer need to live your life desperate for her love. You will be free.

You know, since Columbus discovered America, there have been 65,552 persons who have contributed biologically to your existence. You have had 65,552 "grandparents" since then. And all but four of these you share with your parents. Your mother is just the last in a long line of ancestors, and she shares most of them in common with you! She is just a fellow human being, though perhaps with a very special place in your heart.

Before Columbus arrived, and to this day, there is a tribe of Indians living in Colombia, the Kogi. By the good fortune of geography, civilization has made few inroads into the life and ways of the Kogi, and they appreciate this, constructing elaborate obstacles against intrusions. Some "moderns" have gotten through and have been taught a lovely philosophy of life which describes our relationship to earth and nature and the universe. The word they have for God is mother. They constantly refer to "mother." Mother wants us to be kind to one another; mother wants us to rotate the crops. When pushed for a definition they say that mother is "the mind inside nature." The Kogi recognize that what we hold on to so frantically in our biological mothers is really the purview of the higher power. They even give that power its proper name. We are all, mother and ourselves, children of this mother, the mind inside nature.

That mother cooperates with us. She is mysterious, but she lets our spirits, unique person that each of us is, continue to be born of the mire of our past experience. She lets our spirits emerge. When we live in this wisdom place, the world simply works better. The help that appears for us seemingly out of nowhere seems miraculous. It is just that we become open to more of the infinite reality, both within and without. No longer deafened and blinded by fusion, we hear what our spirits are trying to tell us. We see more of the universe, as it is.

Thank you for staying with me. It's time to go our separate ways. We will probably never meet, but I know that you are struggling to become yourself as I am and as countless others are, all over the world. We are all in this together, and I send my love and encouragement and congratulations to each of you wherever you are. May mother, the mind inside nature, embrace all of her daughters and sons in love and peace and joy, and may we love her back.

Be well.

Afterword

ON THOSE DAYS I jog I prefer to run around the city streets. I enjoy the parks, too, but people are more interesting, changeable. There are some regularities, particularly if I run at the same time, but there is always something different, unpredictable. An older man stands in front of a bus and stops it from proceeding while he signals a cabbie to cut in front of the bus and pick him up. In a generous gesture he gives a smile and a final salute to the bus driver. A young lady in a school uniform puffs on a cigarette while laughing with some other girls and a young man, exploring this new dimension of life.

Young mothers hustle their wee charges, shirts hanging out of their pants, to the nearby nursery school. Men of all ages walk briskly down the avenue, with wasp fedoras and camel hair coats.

I marvel at how busy everybody seems to be, and it dawns on me that this is how we get through our lives without thinking too much about death. Even though we know about it, suffer from it, and even think about it glancingly, we are, most of us, much too busy to dwell on it. So we all go about life in denial, in a sense, of the strange fact that one day we are here and one day we are not. Everyone.

We who are not so busy face certain challenges in keeping the reality of the grim reaper at bay. We have more time, and all things being equal, we are closer to the strange truth that one day we are here and one day we are not. I think this is one of the resistances to "retirement." Instead of this quarter being a time of adventure and freedom and opportunity to learn all sorts of things about life and about ourselves that we never had time to find out, just like all these folks frantically running around on all

90

sides of me as I jog, we get stuck on the fear of the unknown, the grief of impending loss, the anger that Edna St. Vincent Millay expressed when she said, "Death, I'll give you that, but not one thing more." Or Dylan Thomas saying to his dying father: "Do not go gentle into that good night. Rage, rage against the dying of the light." At least they were engaging the issue somewhat, although they may have done a better job of it if they were not drowning themselves in ethyl alcohol.

There are a zillion ways that we avoid a "skillful" (as the Buddhists would say) involvement with "It." Some of us keep on working, perhaps even harder; some lull themselves to sleep by reviewing the current value of their holdings; some replace financially remunerative activity with another compulsive activity. Some of us drive our children crazy by over-involvement or make participation in our grandchildren's lives an obligation rather than a sweet joy. Some go to church more, almost like investing in a good condo in the next place we'll arrive at. But most of us *deny*, cut off our introspective capacities so as not to feel the feelings that accompany the realization of our being here one day and not the next. We leave before our time.

I say this with no criticism. Death is the cruelest event we humans have to deal with and we are the only species that has to endure it. Cut yourself and all of us a lot of slack on this one. It is in a sense impossible. But we humans make a go of it, at times a real good go, and this attempt, in my opinion, is what makes human beings so magnificent.

So don't say goodbye before your time. In fact, never say goodbye. Say hello to life each moment until there is not a moment. We will only die on one day and at one moment. And at that moment I hope for you and me that we are saying hello. Perhaps we can stop calling it names and just realize that one day we will say hello and at some point or another we will not say hello. But never say goodbye, never.

Breinigsville, PA USA
12 October 2009
225590BV00002B/4/P